THE FAMILY EMERGENCY HANDBOOK

Playmore Inc., Publishers
and Waldman Publishing Corp.,
New York, N.Y.

This book is not meant to be used in place of a doctor. It is not meant to substitute for medical help. It is to guide you in aiding someone who needs help until you can get emergency medical attention. In any emergency where medical help is needed, you must get professional assistance as quickly as possible.

The publishers thank Dr. Marcus L. Martin, Professor and Chairman of the Department of Emergency Medicine, University of Virginia, for his medical editing and many other valuable contributions to this book.

Published by Playmore Inc., Publishers,
230 Fifth Avenue, New York, N.Y. 10001
and Waldman Publishing Corp.,
570 Seventh Avenue, New York, N.Y. 10018

Printed in Canada

TABLE OF CONTENTS

THE FAMILY EMERGENCY HANDBOOK

INTRODUCTION

Emergencies happen at home, school, picnics, parties, in our normal, everyday lives. We all hear the unfortunate stories of accidents that may have been prevented or handled better. Families come to emergency departments and frequently say "if only I knew what to do to help" or "I should have known the risk." Simple planning can help you avoid unexpected emergencies.

Having basic knowledge for handling emergencies can help you stay calm and assist until emergency help arrives. All you need are some easy to remember safety tips, first aid supplies, and awareness toward injury prevention. Standard safety precautions can make all the difference to an injured person.

Emergency nurses educate communities, adults and children to prevent injuries, but your help is needed. Once you are aware of how safety helps, you can play a vital role as well. After reading this handbook, continue to learn in this area — read pamphlets and magazines in offices, hospitals, schools and clinics. You can help with a health fair, give classroom talks and share with family and friends.

Contact the Emergency Nurses Association for brochures on injury prevention, alcohol/drug use, proper use of car seats and bicycle helmet use. Make a difference today and every day!

Donna Nowakowski, MS, RN, CAE
Executive Director
EMERGENCY NURSES ASSOCIATION
915 Lee Street
Des Plaines, IL 60016
800/243-8362
enainfo@ena.org
www.ena.org

1 IN CASE OF ILLNESS OR ACCIDENT

YOUR FIRST-AID KIT

Keep these supplies together in a clean, dry container. Place the container where it is easy for you to reach, but where small children will not be able to get at it. Check the kit often and replace any missing supplies promptly. Also put a first-aid kit in your car.

- Sterile first-aid dressing
- Large sterile dressings
- Rolled gauze bandages
- Compression bandage
- Triangular bandage
- 8 safety pins
- 1 roll adhesive tape, 1 inch wide
- Sterile gauze pads
- 1 roll absorbent cotton
- Adhesive bandages, assorted sizes
- 2 elastic bandages, 2-4 inches wide
- Butterfly bandages, assorted sizes
- Cotton-tipped swabs
- Sterile eye wash
- Disposable moist towels for hand-cleansing, sealed in airtight packages
- 6 tongue depressors
- Sharp scissors with rounded tips
- Thermometer, rectal for infants and small children, oral for adults and older children
- Mild soap
- Hydrogen peroxide
- Syrup of ipecac and activated charcoal (use only when emergency personnel tell you to)
- Children's aspirin substitute (use only when a doctor tells you to)
- Ice pack and hot water bottle
- Orabase or Orabase B, mouth bandage
- Topical anesthetic with Benzocaine
- Toothache drops with oil of cloves
- 25 paper cups

- 1 flashlight and batteries
- 1 pair of tweezers
- 1 package of splints, long and short board or inflatable type
- 4 oz. of rubbing alcohol
- 1 each of chemical cold and heat packs
- 2 gal. water
- 1 blanket
- 2 large bath towels
- Prescription medicines
- Mask for assist breathing

FIRST AID & LIFESAVING TECHNIQUES

EMERGENCY TELEPHONE CALLS ARE FREE

Call operator (0), 911, EMS or the Poison Control Center, or take the injured or ill person to a hospital ER.

Here's what each of them does:

Operator. Dial 0 and stay on the line. Ask for help.

911 is the local emergency phone number. When you dial 911, a dispatcher will immediately talk to you. You will be asked what you need, like firefighters, police or emergency medical services. If anybody is hurt, ask for the Emergency Medical Service or EMS.

EMS is manned by trained paramedics or emergency medical technicians (EMTs). Sometimes, it's part of the fire or police department. Often, they are local community volunteers. The EMTs will come with an ambulance. When you call, tell the dispatcher your phone number, where you are, any landmarks, the name of the street and any hazards, like spilled gasoline or electric wires down. Be brief and speak slowly. Give the age and sex of who needs help and why: "Woman, 30 years old, in labor." Remember: Don't hang up on the dispatcher. Let the dispatcher hang up first.

Poison Control Center. Call 1-800-222-1222, for automatic routing to your local Poison Control Center. You will get emergency treatment instructions over the phone. Give the name, age and approximate weight of the poisoning victim. Describe the victim's symptoms. Tell them anything you know about the poison: If you can, have the container and label handy when you call. Tell them what first aid you've already given.

ER stands for Emergency Room. Made famous by TV, this is the hospital department with doctors and nurses specializing in emergencies. Keep your local ER phone number handy. Call ahead if you're coming with somebody who needs help. Tell why they need help: "Five-year-old bitten by dog!" If you have time, take along insurance or Medicare ID, or a credit card. ER is not a free service.

Fill out the charts on the inside covers of this book, keeping family history and the phone numbers for your family doctor and dentist handy. Even if it's after office hours, they may have a 24-hour answering service that will switch you to an emergency number.

CHECKLIST OF IMMEDIATE MEASURES

Treat the most dangerous and urgent condition first. Remember the four B's: breathing, bleeding, broken bones, and burns.

1. Make sure injured person is breathing. If he is not, begin assist breathing immediately. Watch and use caution if person is not known to you. Use mask if available.
2. If breathing is satisfactory, see whether he is bleeding. If the bleeding is heavy, control it immediately.
3. When breathing is satisfactory and there is no sign of bleeding, look for signs of shock and fractured bones.
4. Obtain medical aid quickly.
5. Work quickly, but carefully.
6. Loosen tight clothing, collar and belt.
7. If the victim vomits, lower his head and turn it gently to one side.
8. Remove any loose objects like dentures from the mouth of an unconscious person.
9. Keep victim quiet and warm. Don't overheat.
☞DON'T give an unconscious person anything to drink.
☞DON'T aggravate an injury by unnecessary movements.
☞DON'T urge an injured person to sit up, stand up or walk.

This book is primarily for family emergencies, but you may have to help in an emergency outside your own household. If so, be sure to:

☞Get trained medical emergency people at once. Call 911 or the local Emergency Medical Service (EMS), so they'll be on their way while you're helping out. If there are people with first aid or CPR training already at the site, offer to help, but be aware of your limitations. P.S. If you haven't taken American Red Cross first aid or CPR training, it's a good idea. Look up the American Red Cross in your phone book.
☞Get permission to help. If the person doesn't want your assistance, call for EMS and wait with the person. If the injured person is under age 18, you'll need permission from a parent or guardian (obtaining consent).

☛Stay out of danger. Don't put yourself in harm's way. It is good to assist at an emergency, but don't become a victim yourself!

☛Be careful of the risk of infection. The American Red Cross suggests that you avoid direct contact with blood and saliva. Use disposable latex gloves, a clean cloth, a bandage or even plastic wrap between you and the wound. Always wash your hands with soap and water immediately after providing first aid.

MAKING YOUR HOME SAFE AGAINST ACCIDENTS

Carbon Monoxide (CO)

This deadly gas comes from cars, furnaces, fireplaces and stoves. It can make you very sick or even be fatal.

- Put carbon monoxide alarms near each sleeping area and on each floor of your home.
- If you smell gas or if an alarm goes off, open the doors and windows, and get out of the building right away and call 911.
- Do not touch a light switch, pick up a telephone or make any electrical connection that could create a spark. If you need light, use a flashlight.
- Report the leak to your gas company or your gas supplier from a neighbor's telephone or from a cellphone when you're outside.
- Turn off any appliance or heater that smells funny, starts sooting or has a different looking flame.
- Keep anything made of wood, paper and cloth away from heating appliances.
- Never use charcoal grills inside your home.
- Never warm up a vehicle inside the garage.
- Make sure chimneys are clean and working right.
- Don't use unvented kerosene or gas heaters or a vent-free gas fireplace while sleeping.
- Never use the kitchen stove or oven to heat your home.
- Always turn on the kitchen exhaust fan when using the oven.

Hazardous Household Products

- Never mix products unless the label says it is safe to do it.
- Keep children and pets away from the area while you use hazardous products.
- Always put the cap back on and put the product away right after you finish using it.
- Never leave the product or container where children can see it or reach it.
- Don't eat, drink or smoke when using hazardous products.
- Store hazardous household products in the package, can or bottle they came in. Never put them in another container (especially one for food or drink)! Keep containers and packages dry. Close them tightly.
- Keep products away from heat, sparks or fire.
- Never burn hazardous wastes in a barrel or stove.
- Buy products in childproof containers.
- Find a safe storage area for cleaning products out of the reach of children

and pets — not a cabinet where food supplies are kept. Return products to this storage area immediately after use.
- Never leave a cleaning product near a small child's reach.

Pesticides

These are things like bug spray, bug repellent, pet flea collars and rat poison.
- Always wash your hands after using pesticides.
- Never smoke, eat or drink while using a pesticide.
- Wash clothing you wore while using a pesticide in a separate load from other laundry.
- Mix pesticides outdoors or in an area with plenty of fresh air. (Never mix them inside the kitchen.)
- Follow the directions on the label for the right way to throw away pesticides.
- When putting bug repellent on children, read all directions first. Don't use over cuts or broken skin. Don't apply to eyes, mouth, hands or directly on the face.
- Keep out of the reach of children and pets.

Prevent Slips, Trips & Falls

- Pick up hazards such as toys, shoes and magazines.
- Clean up spills right away so people won't slip.
- Repair any stairs that are cracked or worn.
- Keep your home well lit so you can see where you're walking at night.
- Don't use chairs or tables as makeshift ladders.
- Teach your children not to run indoors or jump down stairs.

Kitchen

- Drain openers, detergents, oven cleaners and other cleaners can hurt you and your children.
- Use a dry chemical or foam fire extinguisher approved for fires ranked Class B (grease and other flammable liquids) and Class C (electrical).
- Keep a fire blanket in the kitchen for flare-ups.

Bathroom

- Put a safety latch on your medicine chest.
- Store medicines in child-safe packaging.
- Don't use space heaters, hair dryers or radios near water.
- Use nonslip mats on bathroom floor and in the shower

Prevent Fires and Burns

- Put in a smoke alarm on every floor of your home in or near every sleeping area.
- Store matches and lighters in a locked drawer.
- Don't let children play near the stove or grill.
- Plan and practice a fire escape route with your family. Do this at night and with the lights off so you'll be ready if there is a fire.
- Keep space heaters out of doorways, halls, or other busy areas.

Other Safety Hints
- Never let children ride on equipment such as lawn tractors.
- Store guns unloaded and locked up.
- Inspect a ladder before climbing it. Look for cracks, bends and wobbling.
- Cover electric outlets.
- Don't use more than 2 plugs in an outlet.
- Make sure old electric cords aren't worn.
- Staircases or landings in apartment houses are not safe for playing.
- Put nonslip webbing under all rugs.

ASSIST BREATHING

Emergency treatment if victim stops breathing

WHAT YOU SHOULD DO

1. Ask person, "Are you okay?"

   a. If person doesn't answer, yell, "Help!" to get somebody to call 911 or operator (0) or EMS.

   b. If you don't think there is a head, back or neck injury, place the person so that you can check for breathing.

   c. Lay the person flat on a firm surface and gently tilt the head back to open airway.

2. Kneel by person's side next to the person's neck and shoulders.

   a. Gently raise chin, and tilt head back.

3. If you think there might be a head, back or neck injury, don't tilt or move person's body or head.

4. Check for breathing. Place your cheek near person's mouth. See if chest rises and falls. Listen for any sounds of breathing. Feel for air on your cheek and ear.

5. If you have a breathing mask available, place it on the person's face and use as directed.

6. If no mask is available, pinch person's nose closed with your fingers. Place your mouth over person's mouth, making a leak-proof seal. Watch and use caution to avoid saliva if the person is not known to you.

7. Take a deep breath.

   a. Breathe into person's mouth, slowly giving two full breaths. Each breath you give should be for at least 1 to 1-1/2 seconds.

   b. Allow for person's natural breathing in between. After each breath, pull your mouth away and take a deep breath yourself. Let air escape from the person's mouth. Stop breathing into person's mouth if you see chest rising.

8. If there's no sign of breathing, gently move person's head. Bend his neck back farther.

   a. Lift the chin higher. Try again.

9. Check person's breathing.

   a. See if his chest rises and falls or if he coughs.

10. Check both sides of throat for pulse.

11. If person is still unconscious, keep giving a breath every four seconds, until help arrives.

12. If person's chest doesn't rise, check for airway blockage. (See below.)

Feeling for a pulse

AIRWAY BLOCKAGE (OBSTRUCTION)

WHAT YOU SHOULD DO

1. Place the victim on his or her back.

   a. Support the neck while moving him into position. Don't move victim if you think the head, neck or back may be injured

2. Lift the neck and tilt the forehead backward.

   a. Then lift the chin upward. This lifts the tongue away from the back of the throat and helps to enlarge the airway. Don't lift or bend the neck if you think it might be hurt by being moved.

3. Push the chin upward without moving the neck.

   a. Listen for breathing by placing your ear near the mouth. At the same time, watch the chest for signs of movement.

4. If the victim is breathing, roll him carefully onto his side. Don't move person if you think their head, neck or back may be injured.

5. If there is no sign of breathing or breathing isn't strong enough, open the mouth and pass your finger beyond tongue to remove any foreign material like false teeth, food, or vomit.

If person's chest doesn't rise, check for airway blockage.

Assist breathing

WHAT YOU SHOULD NOT DO

☛ **DON'T** move victim if you think their head, neck or back may be injured.

☛ **DON'T** stop assist breathing for more than 15 seconds, until the person is breathing on his own.

CHOKING

This happens when the airway is blocked, and the victim can't breathe. A swallowed object is often the cause. This may happen when the victim is talking and eating at the same time.

WHAT TO LOOK FOR
- Victim can't breathe
- Victim can't speak or cry out
- May use universal sign of choking (grabbing at throat or neck)
- Turns blue or even purple
- Eyes bulge
- Collapses
- Becomes unconscious

Ask victim, "Are you choking?"

Universal sign of choking

WHAT YOU SHOULD DO

If Victim is Conscious, Sitting or Standing

A conscious victim will usually point to his/her mouth or hold his/her neck, trying to show an airway problem.

1. Ask the victim these questions:

- "Are you choking?"
- "Can you speak?"
- "Can you cough?"

2. If the answer is "Yes," there is a partial obstruction (blockage).

   a. Tell the victim to cough. A strong and forceful cough shows that the victim is breathing enough air to maintain consciousness. Don't interfere with the victim's attempts to clear his airway by coughing.

   b. When the victim may have a weak cough or is turning blue or gray, treat the victim as if his airway is completely blocked.

3. If there is a complete airway blockage, perform the Heimlich maneuver.

   a. Stand behind the victim and place your arms around the victim's waist.

4. Make a fist with one hand

   a. Grasp one fist in your other hand.

   b. Put the thumb side of your fist against the middle of the victim's abdomen just above the navel and well below rib cage.

   c. Don't squeeze victim.

5. Press your fist into the victim's abdominal area with five quick upward thrusts.

6. If airway is still blocked, keep doing it.

12

If Victim Becomes Unconscious

7. Shout, "Help!" Tell somebody to call 911 or operator (0) or EMS.

8. Don't let victim fall. Catch him. Let him slowly slide down to floor, face up. Make sure his head does not hit floor.

9. Get any foreign object out of his mouth.

   a. Place your thumb in victim's mouth over tongue. Caution: Watch out for biting and saliva. Cuts can become infected.

   b. Wrap fingers around jaw and lift tongue and jaw upward.

10. While holding tongue and jaw, use other hand to remove any foreign object in victim's mouth. Use your finger to get the object out.

11. Do assist breathing. (See page 10.)

12. Give abdominal thrusts.

   a. Sit on top of victim's thighs and place heel of your hand on victim's stomach just above navel and well below ribcage.

   b. Place other hand on top of that hand. Fingers of both hands should point to victim's head.

   c. Push upwards ten times.

13. Keep repeating steps 9 through 12 until object is loosened and victim is breathing or until emergency help arrives.

14. Do not put objects such as spoons in victim's mouth.

Take out anything in the mouth.

1. Remove whatever is in the mouth of an unconscious victim. Use your fingers.

2. Open the victim's mouth with one hand.

3. Clear the blockage with other hand. Use your index finger to hook and remove any object inside his mouth.

13

DROWNING

WHAT TO LOOK FOR
- Lips and fingernails turn bluish
- Breathing stops
- Unconsciousness

WHAT YOU SHOULD DO
1. Get medical help right away. Call 911 or operator (0) or EMS.

Until help comes:

2. If victim is near the shore or the side of a swimming pool, lie down at the water edge.

   a. Give him/her your hand or foot and pull to safety.

3. If victim is not near, reach out with something like a rope, pole or board.

   a. Carry victim to safety.

4. Keep his head lower than the rest of body when carrying him.

5. Lay victim on back on a coat or blanket.

6. Open airway.

   a. Give assist breathing if needed. (See page 10.)

7. Take off wet clothing.

8. Keep victim warm.

If victim is not near, reach out with a rope, pole or board of some kind.

WHAT YOU SHOULD NOT DO
☛ **DON'T** move victim after rescue if you think their head, neck or back may be injured.

Rescue from drowning

CARBON MONOXIDE (CO) POISONING

Caused by bad gas heater, blocked chimney flue or exhaust of car or truck. Because carbon monoxide (CO) does not have an odor, you can be affected without knowing it. A carbon monoxide (CO) alarm in your home will warn you if this gas is present. Plug in carbon monoxide alarms wherever carbon monoxide fumes may build up: the kitchen, garage, or near a fireplace. Carbon monoxide alarms are sold in hardware stores.

WHAT TO LOOK FOR

Get outside right away.

- Shortness of breath
- Coughing
- Headache
- Dizziness
- Yawning
- Fainting
- Weakness
- Nausea and/or vomiting

WHAT YOU SHOULD DO

1. If someone in your family shows signs of CO poisoning or if a CO alarm goes off, get outside right away.

2. Get medical help right away. Call 911 or operator (0) or EMS.

Until help comes:

3. As soon as it's safe (first let gas escape from room), move the victim to fresh air as quickly as possible.

4. Open his airway. Use assist breathing. (See page 10.)

5. Treat the victim for shock. (See page 38.)

6. Stay with victim until help arrives.

WHAT YOU SHOULD NOT DO

☞ **DON'T** enter a gas-filled room without proper safety equipment.

HEAVY BLEEDING FROM WOUNDS

There are different kinds of wounds that may cause bleeding. This list may help you describe the wound clearly when you call 911.

- Abrasions or scrapes are caused by rubbing or scraping.
- Lacerated wounds have rough or jagged edges.
- Puncture wounds are produced by pointed objects.
- Incised wounds are caused by a sharp cutting edge, such as a knife or razor.
- An avulsion tears a whole piece of skin and tissue loose or leaves it hanging as a flap.
- Amputation — a body part such as a leg or arm is completely cut through or torn off.
- Crush injuries can result when a part of the body is caught between heavy pieces of equipment or machinery.

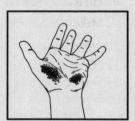

Abrasion

WHAT TO LOOK FOR

- A lot of bright-red or dark-red blood is coming out fast from a cut or wound.
- The victim may be hurting a lot.
- The black pupils in the center of the eye have gotten big.
- Skin feels damp, cool and wet.
- Skin looks blotchy.
- Heart beat or pulse is fast but weak.
- Breathing is also fast, like a runner panting.
- Victim may throw up.
- Victim is thirsty.
- Victim may not know what's going on.
- Victim may be weak and can't get up.
- Victim may be woozy, even sleepy, may even pass out (faint).

Incision

WHAT YOU SHOULD DO

1. Call 911, the operator (0) or the Emergency Medical Service (EMS).

Until help comes:

2. Have the victim lie down.

3. If there's no broken bone, elevate the bleeding part if it's an arm or leg.

4. Keep the victim warm with a blanket.

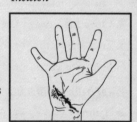

Laceration

Puncture wound

5. Wash your own hands and then clean the wound of any large pieces of dirt or debris. Put on disposable latex gloves if you have them.

6. Cover the wound. Here's how:

   a. Make a pad of clean and thick cloth. Use gauze from a first-aid kit. If you don't have gauze, use a clean undershirt, towel, bedsheet or handkerchief.

   b. Put it over the place where the blood is coming from.

   c. Make sure it covers the entire wound.

7. Press your hand right over the dressing. (Anything put over a wound is called a "dressing.")

8. When the dressing gets soaked with blood, replace with another dry, clean padded cloth.

9. Press down for five minutes.

10. If the bleeding doesn't stop, hold down on a pressure point. Pressure points of the arm are on the inside of the arm just above the elbow and just below the armpit. Pressure points of the leg are just behind the knee and in the groin.

    a. Press down on the pressure point for only a few minutes.

11. Don't stop pressing on the wound. Press down on both the pressure point and the wound.

12. When bleeding starts to slow down, let up on the pressure point.

13. When bleeding stops altogether, you can then make a bandage. This keeps the dressing in place. If you don't have first-aid tape, use a necktie, belt or strips of cloth — anything that will hold the dressing over the wound.

14. Keep the victim quiet and lying still. Reassure the victim.

WHAT YOU SHOULD **NOT** DO

☞ If there's a bone sticking out of the wound, **DON'T** press on top of the wound. Instead, press down around it.

Watch for shock. This can happen if the victim loses a lot of blood.

Injured Hand

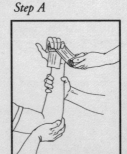
Step A

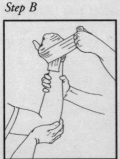
Step B

SMALL WOUNDS

WHAT TO LOOK FOR

- Tiny bleeding spots, "shaving nicks," scratches, small cuts
- It might be swollen (puffy)

WHAT YOU SHOULD DO

1. If cut is long and deep, first call 911 or operator (0) or EMS.

2. Wash your own hands.

   a. Gently scrub wound with soap and water so that all the dirt you see is washed out. Try to keep soap out of the wound itself. It can irritate the injury.

   b. Rinse under running water for at least 10 minutes.

   c. If you have disposable latex gloves put them on.

3. If there's no broken bone, raise the bleeding body part higher than the heart.

4. Cover the wound. Keep it dry.

   a. Put clean and thick cloth (compress) over the place where the blood is coming from.

   b. Use the cleanest material you can find. Use a gauze pad or a germ-free sterile dressing (covering that's placed right over a wound) from a first-aid kit. In a pinch you can also use any cloth that's clean: a towel, a bed sheet, an undershirt, a napkin or a freshly laundered handkerchief.

   c. Put the clean dressing right over the wound. Don't let it touch anything else.

   d. For long bone wounds (shin, forearm), use a spiral bandage. Wind bandage around limb.

5. Press your hand right over the dressing.

6. When the material gets soaked with blood, replace with another dry, clean padded cloth.

7. Press down for five minutes.

8. Keep pressing until bleeding stops or slows.

9. Keep injured area up.

10. If bandage becomes wet, remove it and put on a new one.

WHAT YOU SHOULD <u>NOT</u> DO

☞ **DON'T** ignore any signs of infection. These may include
- swelling, puffiness
- throbbing pain
- redness
- pus
- swollen glands in the neck, armpit or groin
- heat
- fever
- red streaks leading from the wound.

Don't ignore any signs of infection.

If you see any of these signs of infection, get victim to a doctor or the emergency room of a hospital quickly.

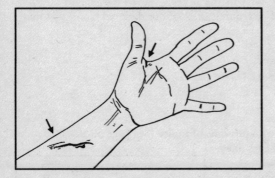

Bleeding

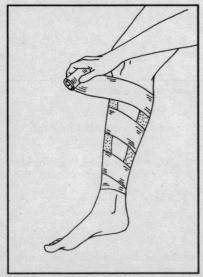

Spiral bandage step 1

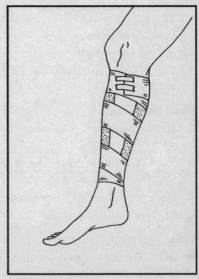

Spiral bandage step 2

HEAVY BLEEDING INSIDE THE BODY (CLOSED WOUNDS)

This is when something inside has been hurt, but the skin may not have been torn or cut.

WHAT TO LOOK FOR *(You may not see every sign.)*

- A bruise or wound on the neck
- Head feels sore
- Bleeding from a chest wound
- A broken pelvis, thighbone or upper arm
- A swollen, tender, stiff or bruised abdomen
- Bleeding from the ears, mouth, nose or other body openings
- Coughing up bright red blood
- Blood in the urine
- Bright red blood or dark, tarry matter in feces (bowel movement)
- Vomit that looks like coffee grounds or bright or dark red blood that may be all bubbly
- Fast or panting breathing
- Breathing may stop altogether
- Eyes may be dull, without brightness
- Blurred eyesight
- Dizziness standing up
- Feeling weak and helpless
- Showing signs of shock without signs of injury (See page 38.)
- Black pupils in center of eyes dilate (dark and large center)
- Skin may feel cold or clammy
- Skin may turn pale, gray or bluish
- Thirstiness
- Yawning or sighing

Calm the injured victim.

Cover with a blanket

WHAT YOU SHOULD DO

1. Call 911, the operator (0) or EMS right away.

Until help comes:

2. If breathing stops, give assist breathing or mouth-to-mouth. (See page 10.)

3. Put a splint on any injured arm or leg that may be bleeding on the inside. (See page 49 for splints.)

4. Cover any wounds. Cover victim with blanket.

5. Calm the injured victim.

WHAT YOU SHOULD <u>NOT</u> DO

- ☛ **DON'T** move victim if you think their head, neck or back may be injured.
- ☛ **DON'T** give victim anything to eat or drink.

20

BACK AND NECK INJURIES

These can be very serious. If you think back or neck has been hurt, do not move the victim. Wait for emergency professionals.

WHAT TO LOOK FOR
- Pain in the head, neck or back
- Can't feel arms or legs
- Can't move arms or legs
- Loss of bladder or bowel control
- Numbness

WHAT YOU SHOULD DO
1. Get medical help right away. Call 911 or operator (0) or EMS.

Until help comes:

2. Do not move victim. This is very important!

3. Keep victim warm.

WHAT YOU SHOULD NOT DO
☛ **DON'T** move victim.

INJURIES TO THE NOSE AND OBJECTS IN THE NOSE

NOSEBLEEDS

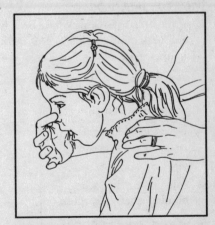

Nosebleed

WHAT TO LOOK FOR
- Bleeding
- Pain
- Trouble breathing

WHAT YOU SHOULD DO
1. Control the bleeding. Victim should sit down and lean slightly forward, keeping mouth open. Have him hold his head so that blood does not drain into the throat. If victim can't sit down, lay him/her down with head slightly raised or turn the head to one side.

2. Gently pinch the nostrils closed with thumb and index finger. You or the victim, if old enough, can do this.

   a. Pinch nostrils together at lower part of nose, the soft portion below the

21

bone, for about 15 minutes. Release slowly.

3. Place cold cloth or ice wrapped in a towel against nose.

4. If bleeding continues, put a small pad of gauze in one nostril, and pinch it closed for another five minutes.

5. Keep pinching the nostrils until bleeding is stopped.

6. Tell victim to try not to blow nose or bend head.

7. If nose keeps bleeding, call doctor or EMS.

8. It's important to let your doctor know about nosebleeds.

9. Call 911, the operator (0) or EMS immediately if you think there's a chance of head or neck injury.

WHAT YOU SHOULD *NOT* DO

☞ **DON'T** move victim if you think their head, neck or back may be injured.

INJURED OR BROKEN NOSE

WHAT TO LOOK FOR

- Pain in nose
- Breathing difficulty

Don't try to splint nose.

WHAT YOU SHOULD DO

1. If the neck or back may have been hurt, DON'T move victim. (See back and neck injuries, page 21.) If the head may have been injured, see head injuries, page 24.

2. Stop the bleeding. Use two fingers to pinch nostrils shut at lower part of nose.

3. Place cold cloth or ice wrapped in towel over nose.

4. Bring victim to doctor or hospital emergency room.

WHAT YOU SHOULD *NOT* DO

☞ **DON'T** try to splint nose.

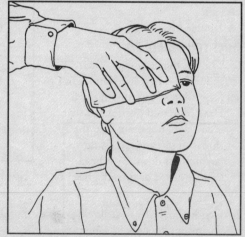

Broken Nose

PUNCTURE WOUNDS, INCLUDING SPLINTERS

Something sharp has gone through the skin. It can be a splinter, staple, tack, nail or a pencil or piece of wire.

WHAT TO LOOK FOR

- Foreign body
- Pain
- Little bleeding

Watch for signs of infection.

WHAT YOU SHOULD DO

1. Call 911, the operator (0) or EMS if something large like a nail has gone through the skin.

2. Scrub your hands clean.

3. If it's a splinter, you can try to remove it with clean tweezers. Wiping or dipping in rubbing alcohol may help to clean tweezers. Carefully pull out the splinter if it's not deeply stuck in the skin.

4. Wash out the wound with running water.

5. Cover the wound with a sterile dressing (germ-free cloth). Keep the cloth in place with a bandage. If topical antibiotic ointment is on hand, and the person has no known allergy to it, it may be applied.

6. Watch for signs of infection. These may include swelling, puffiness, throbbing pain, redness, pus, swollen glands in the neck, armpit or groin, heat, fever or red streaks leading from the wound.

   a. If you see any of these signs of infection or you're unable to remove the splinter or bleeding is uncontrollable, get victim to a doctor or the emergency room of a hospital quickly.

WHAT YOU SHOULD NOT DO

☞ **DON'T** try to remove large objects from a puncture wound.
☞ **DON'T** poke around in wound.

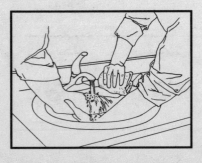

Cleanse puncture wounds

HEAD INJURIES

This could be a bump on the head from a fall. It also includes skull fractures or brain injury, so call 911 or EMS right away.

WHAT TO LOOK FOR

Don't try to remove any objects that may be in head.

- Lump, wound, cut, or soft spot on the scalp
- Pain in head
- Unconsciousness, blackouts
- Sleepiness or confusion
- Bleeding from the nose, ear, or mouth
- Fluid coming out of the nose or ears
- Vomiting
- Convulsions, "the shakes," fit or seizure
- Discoloration under the eyes, like "black eyes."
- The black pupils in the center of the eyes are of different sizes
- Finding it hard to breathe
- Can't move arms or legs
- Can't talk, or finds it hard to talk
- Restlessness

WHAT YOU SHOULD DO

1. Call 911 or operator (0) or EMS.

Until help comes:

2. If victim cannot move arms, hands, fingers, legs, feet, or toes, or has pain in neck or back, don't move victim. See back and neck injuries, page 21.

3. Check breathing. If breathing stops, do assist breathing. (See page 10.)

4. Keep victim lying down and quiet.

5. If you don't think there's a back or neck injury, raise head and shoulders slightly with a pillow, blanket or rolled towel. Turn victim's head to side. Don't try to remove any objects that may be in head.

6. Control bleeding with a pressure bandage. Place clean cloth compress over minor head wounds, and tie down with strips of cloth or bandages.

WHAT YOU SHOULD NOT DO

☛ **DON'T** give victim anything to eat or drink.
☛ **DON'T** move victim if you think their neck or back may be injured.

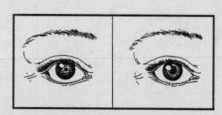

Pupils are different sizes

SCALP WOUNDS

These cuts or scrapes on the top of the head may bleed a lot.

WHAT TO LOOK FOR

- Shock
- Unconsciousness (passes out)
- Heavy bleeding
- Dizziness
- Nausea
- Mild headache
- Loss of memory (forgetfulness)

Check for other injuries to the head at the same time.

WHAT YOU SHOULD DO

1. Scalp wounds bleed a lot, so they should be bandaged carefully.

    a. Check for other injuries to the head at the same time. If victim is dizzy, can't remember what happened, faints or passes out, call 911, the operator (0) or the EMS.

2. Cover the scalp injury with a piece of gauze or a large bandage compress from a first-aid kit. You can also use a clean towel, or laundered bed sheet, undershirt, or another piece of clean cloth.

3. Press firmly but gently to stop bleeding.

    a. If dressing gets soaked with blood, replace with another dry, clean padded bandage.

4. Keep pressing until bleeding stops.

5. Bandage it in place with an elastic roller bandage, which goes around the head.

6. See a doctor.

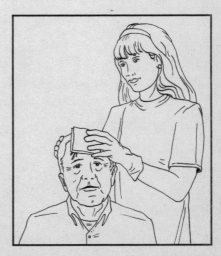

Press clean pad on scalp wound

NECK WOUNDS

WHAT TO LOOK FOR

- Wound in the neck
- Bright red or dark red (maroon) blood
- Headache
- Stiff neck

Don't try to move victim.

WHAT YOU SHOULD DO

1. Get medical help right away. Call 911, operator (0) or EMS. Tell the dispatcher if the victim can't move arms or legs, or has back or neck pain.

Until help comes:

2. If breathing stops, use assist breathing. (See page 10.)

3. Apply a dressing (cloth pad) to the wound. If you have germ-free (sterile) dressings in your first-aid kit, use those. Otherwise, make a pad of and place on the wound any clean material — cloth, toweling, laundered bed-sheets, T-shirt — that will extend two inches beyond the wound.

4. Firmly but gently press your hand over the dressing to stop the bleeding.

   a. If blood soaks material, replace it with another clean cloth.

5. When bleeding has stopped, bandage the dressing in place.

6. Keep victim lying down. Don't move victim.

WHAT YOU SHOULD _NOT_ DO

☛ **DON'T** try to move victim.

CHEST WOUNDS

WHAT TO LOOK FOR

- Something sticking out of the chest, like a knife or screwdriver. ("A penetrating chest wound")
- Blood coming out of the chest that is bubbly or foamy. ("A sucking chest wound")
- Difficulty breathing

WHAT YOU SHOULD DO

Make sure victim is breathing.

1. Get medical help right away. Call 911, the operator (0) or EMS.

Until help comes:

2. DON'T try to remove anything sticking out of the chest.

3. Make sure victim is breathing. (See assist breathing, page 10.)

4. Over the wound, put a large piece of folded clean cloth, or a sterile gauze pad from your first-aid kit, or a clean towel, pillowcase or undershirt.

5. Cover the wound and two inches all around it.

6. Try to make sure the covering is snug to keep air from escaping.

7. Cover the dressing with aluminum foil or plastic wrap.

8. Tape the wound shut with adhesive tape or bandages.

WHAT YOU SHOULD <u>NOT</u> DO

- ☞ **DON'T** give victim anything to eat or drink.
- ☞ **DON'T** show panic.

ABDOMINAL INJURIES

The abdomen (middle, belly, stomach) has been hurt in some way.

WHAT TO LOOK FOR
- Cuts, puncture wounds or large bruised area
- A burning feeling
- Pain in stomach, abdomen, middle or lower part of torso
- Coughing up or vomiting blood that looks like coffee grounds
- Rigid (stiff, tense), tender or swollen abdomen
- Legs drawn up

WHAT YOU SHOULD DO
1. Get medical help right away. Call 911, the operator (0) or EMS.

Until help comes:

2. Loosen clothing.

3. Watch for vomiting and keep it out of airway.

4. If breathing stops, use assist breathing. (See page 10.)

5. Lay the victim on his/her back.

   a. If wound goes across abdomen, raise knees gently and support victim.

   b. If wound goes up and down the abdomen, don't raise knees.

6. Fold a large dressing, a towel or clean cloth and put it over the wound.

7. Tape the cloth with tape or a bandage.

8. If cloth dressing gets soaked with blood, replace with another dry, clean cloth pad.

9. Don't touch any part of the intestine that may be out.

10. Cover victim with a blanket.

11. Treat victim for shock. (See page 38.)

In extreme cases, there may be an organ protruding (sticking out).

1. Remove as much clothing around the wound as you can.

2. Don't touch or try to replace the organ.

3. Cover loosely with a moist dressing that extends at least two inches beyond the wound edges or the edges of the exposed organ. Don't use aluminum foil, tissue paper or fluffy materials like cotton balls.

4. If you have it, use tape to seal the moist dressing or plastic wrap in place.

5. Put a thick cloth pad or lint-free towel over the original dressing.

6. Don't try to remove objects that may be sticking in body.

WHAT YOU SHOULD <u>NOT</u> DO
- ☛ **DON'T** move the victim.
- ☛ **DON'T** give any food or water.
- ☛ **DON'T** touch any protruding organs.

AMPLITATION

WHAT TO LOOK FOR
- A missing body part
- Bleeding

WHAT YOU SHOULD DO
1. Get medical help right away. Call 911 or operator (0) or EMS.

Until you get help:

2. Control bleeding by direct pressure. (See page 17.)

3. Raise wounded limb over level of heart.

4. Cover wound with sterile dressing, clean cloth, towel, undershirt, bedsheet, handkerchief or unused sanitary napkin.

5. Press down on dressing until bleeding stops or slows down.

6. Keep injured area raised.

7. If bleeding does not stop or slow down after a couple of minutes of direct pressure and elevation, keep up the direct pressure on wound.

   a. Also push on pressure point between wound and heart. The two most used pressure points are in the upper arm and in the groin.

8. If the wound is in the upper body, press your fingers against the inner side of the upper arm in the groove between muscles.

9. If the wound is in the lower body, press the heel of your hand down where the thigh and groin meet.

10. As soon as bleeding stops, stop pressing on pressure point.

11. When you've controlled bleeding, tie down the dressing with a bandage.

12. Check for signs of shock. (See page 38.)

13. If possible, recover the cut-off body part. Don't wash it or put it in water.

   a. Soak clean gauze with clean water, or use any clean cloth to wrap it in.

   b. Wrap amputated part with the wet gauze or cloth.

   c. Put wrapped amputated body part in a plastic bag or container and give it to emergency personnel when they arrive.

WHAT YOU SHOULD NOT DO
☞ **DON'T** move victim if you think their head, neck or back may be injured.

If possible, recover the severed part of the body.

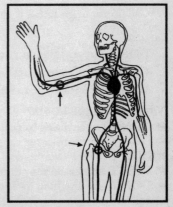

Pressure points

EAR INJURIES AND EARACHES

WHAT TO LOOK FOR
- Bleeding or other fluids (yellow or white) coming from the ear
- Pain
- Hearing loss or deafness
- Ringing in the ears

Don't tap or strike the ear.

WHAT YOU SHOULD DO

General Injuries To The Ear

1. Get medical help right away. Call 911 or operator (0) or EMS.

Until help comes:

2. Don't move person if you think their head, neck or back may be injured.

3. Don't try to stop fluids coming from victim's ear. Don't put anything in ear.

4. If you can't find any back or neck injury, lay victim down on side.

   a. Prop victim's head and shoulders up with a pillow or folded blanket or towels.

Cut On Outer Ear

1. If ear has been cut off, see amputations (page 29).

2. Don't put anything in ear.

3. Press bandage over wound to stop bleeding.

   a. Keep bandage in place by wrapping large cloth or towel around victim's head.

4. Keep victim's head up and go to a hospital ER or doctor.

Object In Ear (including insect)

1. DON'T put anything in ear.

2. Loosely cover ear with clean cloth, towel, or bandage.

3. Tilt person's head towards affected side.

4. Call doctor or go to ER if object doesn't come out.

Earache

1. DON'T put anything in victim's ear.

2. Call doctor or go to ER. This may be a sign of ear infection.

WHAT YOU SHOULD <u>NOT</u> DO
- ☞ DON'T put anything in victim's ear.
- ☞ DON'T tap or strike the ear.
- ☞ DON'T use ice water to cool.
- ☞ DON'T touch a burn or breathe on it.
- ☞ DON'T give anything to drink.

Don't put anything in ear

MOUTH INJURIES

WHAT TO LOOK FOR
- Cuts
- Bleeding
- Teeth broken or knocked out

Don't try to clean knocked-out teeth.

WHAT YOU SHOULD DO

1. Check for head injuries. (See head injuries, page 24, and back and neck injuries, page 21.)

2. Stop the bleeding:

For Lip.

Stop bleeding by pressing on lip from both sides of wound.

For an Injured Tongue.

Stop bleeding by pressing both sides of tongue.

For Gums and Roof of Mouth.

Stop bleeding by pressing on gums or roof of mouth.

For Injuries to Teeth.

1. Stop bleeding by having victim bite down on teabag, cloth or dressing placed on tooth or socket.

2. Remove knocked-out teeth.

   a. Don't try to clean them. Rinse gently in tap water. Wrap in wet cloth or drop into glass of milk, or container of water.

3. Victim should go immediately to doctor or dentist.

WHAT YOU SHOULD NOT DO
☛ **DON'T** try to clean knocked-out teeth.

EYE INJURIES

WHAT TO LOOK FOR

- Bleeding
- Pain
- Redness
- A feeling of "sand in the eye"
- Sensitivity to light
- Tearing
- Something stuck in eye (impalement)
- Chemical in eye
- Object in eye
- Black eye

Eye injuries

WHAT YOU SHOULD DO for:

Something Stuck In Eye (Impalement)

1. Get medical help right away. Call 911, the operator (0) or EMS at once.

Until help comes:

2. Don't let victim touch or rub eye.

3. Don't try to remove object.

4. Tell the victim that both eyes must be covered to protect the injured eye.

5. Cut hole in thick dressing or a folded cloth.

   a. Put a paper cup over injured eye and embedded object. Or make a cone with tape and folded paper and put that over the eye.

   b. Don't touch object or eye.

   c. Hold cup in place with roller bandage from first-aid kit, or use a scarf or towel that covers both eyes.

6. Never leave the victim alone, as the victim may panic with both eyes covered.

Chemical In Eye

1. Get medical help at once. Call 911, or operator (0) or EMS.

Until help comes:

2. Flood hurt eye with clean running water for at least 30 minutes.

3 Hold eyelid open. Pour water slowly over eyeball over INNER corner.

   a. Have victim roll eyeball. This will help wash out eye.

   b. Let water run out from OUTER corner.

c. Don't let water run into the other eye.

4. Don't bandage eye.

Object In Eye

Don't allow victim to touch eye.

1. DON'T let victim rub eye.

2. Wash your hands.

3. Gently pull upper eyelid outward and down over lower eyelid.

   a. Hold for a minute. Tears should flow to wash out foreign object.

4. If particle is not washed out, get victim to a doctor or ER right away.

Cut On Eyeball Or Eyelid

1. Get medical help immediately. Call 911 or operator (0) or EMS.

Until help comes:

For a Cut to Eyeball —

2. Cover both eyes with clean gauze or folded cloth.

3. Hold in place with bandage. Don't press down. Don't let victim touch eye.

For Cut to Eyelid —

4. Gently press lid against bone around eye. This helps stop bleeding.

Black Eye

1. Put an ice-cold compress, ice pack or ice cubes wrapped in a towel, to the area around the eye. Apply ice for 10 minutes.

2. Don't press on the eye.

3. Keep victim lying down.

4. Have him/her close eyes.

5. Get to a doctor if eyesight is blurred, or if there is pain, or bleeding in the eye.

WHAT YOU SHOULD NOT DO

☛ If victim is wearing contact lenses, **DON'T** try to remove them.

☛ **DON'T** press on the eyeball.

☛ **DON'T** rub eye.

BURNS AND SCALDS

WHAT TO LOOK FOR

There are four kinds of burns:

Don't try to break blisters.

- First degree (Minor) — redness.
- Second degree (Moderate) — blisters.
- Third degree (Critical) — deep tissue damage.
- Fourth degree — deep tissue damage and may include bone.

WHAT YOU SHOULD DO FOR:

First And Second Degree Burns

1. For burns larger than the size of a hand, call 911 or operator (0) or EMS.

Until help comes:

2. Stick burned area in cold water (not ice).

   a. Put cold compresses on burn until pain begins to go away. Then blot dry with clean towel, cloth or gauze.

3. Cover burned area with a clean dressing. Then bandage loosely.

4. Elevate burned area if possible.

5. Watch for signs of shock. (See page 38.)

6. Watch for signs of infection (swelling, puffiness, pain, redness, red streaks).

Third And Fourth Degree Burns

1. Get medical help immediately. Call 911 or operator (0) or EMS right away.

Until help comes:

2. Make sure victim is breathing. If breathing has stopped, apply assist breathing. (See page 10.)

3. Cool burned area with cool water.

4. Keep victim laying down.

5. Raise body parts that have been burned. Elevate burned hands.

6. Cover bad burns with clean dry cloth.

WHAT YOU SHOULD NOT DO

- ☛ DON'T use antiseptic sprays, butter, ointment or home remedies.
- ☛ DON'T try to remove clothing that has stuck on.
- ☛ DON'T try to break blisters.
- ☛ DON'T put any pressure on burned area.
- ☛ DON'T make cover bandages tight.
- ☛ DON'T use ice water to cool.
- ☛ DON'T touch a burn or breathe on it.
- ☛ DON'T give anything to drink.

CHEMICAL BURNS

For example, burns from drain cleaner, dishwasher liquids, paint stripper, oven cleaner, strong detergent, caustics and other sources.

WHAT TO LOOK FOR
- Skin is red, blisters and peels
- Painful skin

WHAT YOU SHOULD DO
1. Get medical help right away. Call 911, the operator (0) or EMS.

Until help comes:

2. Brush away any chemical powder. Take off all clothing with chemicals on it.

3 Put victim under shower for 10 minutes. Or use a garden hose or buckets of water.

  a. Then blot victim dry with clean towel, cloth or gauze.

4. Cover burn with a clean bandage or clean cloth.

5. Treat for shock. (See page 38.)

WHAT YOU SHOULD NOT DO
☞ **DON'T** use sprays, ointments or antiseptics.

Flush chemicals away

Burns Of The Eyes By Chemicals

WHAT TO LOOK FOR
- Sharp pain in the eye
- Can't open eye
- Eye is red
- Eye is tearing badly
- Chemicals in the area near victim

WHAT YOU SHOULD DO
1. Get medical help right away. Call 911, or operator (0) or EMS at once.

Until help comes:

2. Have victim lie down.

3. Hold eyelids open with fingers. Make sure fingers are clean.

4. Pour water gently into the inner corner of the eye. Use plenty of water.

   a. Let the water flow into the outer corner.

   b. Don't let the water splash into the other eye.

   c. Wash the eyes for at least 30 minutes.

WHAT YOU SHOULD <u>NOT</u> DO

☛ **DON'T** use any medication or boric acid.

☛ **DON'T** force contact lenses off.

Wash the eyes for at least 30 minutes.

Chemicals on skin

ELECTRICAL INJURIES: BURNS & SHOCK

Electricity, whether high or low voltage, can burn, shock or even kill.

WHAT TO LOOK FOR
- Power source
- Unconscious victim
- Burns

Make sure current is off before touching victim.

WHAT YOU SHOULD DO

1. Look first. Don't touch victim directly who is in contact with electricity.

2. Turn off current.

3. If you must remove victim before turning off current, stand on something dry, such as newspapers, books or phone directories, a blanket, rubber mat or cloth. If you have them, put on rubber gloves.

    a. Use a broomstick handle, a dry plank or a stick to push victim away from electricity. Don't use anything metal.

4. If victim is not breathing, try assist breathing. (See page 10.)

5. Get medical help right away. Call 911 or operator (0) or EMS.

Until help comes:

6. Look for signs of shock. (See page 38.)

7. Treat burns as thermal (heat) burns. (See page 34.)

8. Splint any fractures. (See page 49.)

WHAT YOU SHOULD _NOT_ DO

☛ **DON'T** get shocked or burned yourself. Make sure current is off before touching victim.

☛ **DON'T** move victim if you think their head, neck or back may be injured.

Electric shock

SHOCK

This is a very dangerous condition where there is heavy loss of blood and cells don't get nutrients or oxygen. There are many emergencies where shock has to be treated.

WHAT TO LOOK FOR (not all these signs may be present)
- Sweat (perspiration)
- Blotchy or streaked skin that may also be cold or clammy
- Dazed and confused
- Dull look in eyes
- Fast panting
- Nausea and vomiting
- Pale or bluish lips and fingernails
- Paleness in light skinned people and grayness in dark skinned people
- Restlessness or uneasiness
- Sleepiness, unconsciousness
- Thirst
- Dilated eyes, dark pupils (See page 24.)
- Weak and helpless feeling
- Weak, rapid pulse (heartbeat)

Shock signs

WHAT YOU SHOULD DO
1. Get medical help right away. Call 911 or operator (0) or EMS.

2. If victim is not breathing, use assist breathing. (See page 10.)

3. If you think there may be back, neck or head injury, don't move victim. (See page 21 and page 24.)

4. If there doesn't seem to be any head, back, or neck injury, lay victim face up on blanket.

5. Loosen tight clothing.

6. If there are no injuries to legs or head, raise feet 10 or 12 inches.

7. Check for injuries or bleeding. (See page 7.)

8. Cover victim with blanket or jacket. Keep victim comfortable.

9. If victim throws up, turn victim's head to side if you don't suspect back, head or neck injuries.

10. Check breathing again.

WHAT YOU SHOULD NOT DO
- ☞ **DON'T** give victim anything to eat or drink.
- ☞ **DON'T** move victim if you suspect back, head, or neck injuries.
- ☞ **DON'T** raise feet if legs or feet are broken.

38

ALLERGIC REACTION (ANAPHYLACTIC SHOCK)

This can happen within minutes, sometimes seconds, to some very allergic victims. The airway may swell up, cutting off air. It could be caused by bee stings, a medication, food such as chocolate and nuts, pollen, dust and other allergens.

WHAT TO LOOK FOR

- Blisters
- Cold, clammy skin
- Difficulty in breathing
- Dizziness
- Heavy sneezing and coughing
- Hives (bumps on the skin)
- Itching or burning skin
- Nausea
- Red face
- Swelling of the tongue, ears and face
- Tightening or pain in the chest
- Weak pulse/heartbeat
- Convulsion or fit
- Jitteriness
- Ringing or throbbing in the ears
- Unconsciousness
- Low blood pressure

Check victim's breathing.

WHAT YOU SHOULD DO

1. Get medical help right away. Call 911 or operator (0) or EMS.

Until help comes:

2. If victim has had this allergic reaction before, he or she may have an injection kit.

   a. If there is an injection kit, have victim inject himself/herself.

   b. If they can't, read directions in the kit and give the injection.

3. Check victim's breathing. If victim's breathing has stopped, apply assist breathing. (See page 10.).

4. If there's shortness of breath, have victim sit up. Otherwise, have victim lie down.

5. Put a blanket over victim.

WHAT YOU SHOULD NOT DO

☛ **DON'T** wait to call 911. Do it at once. A quick response to an allergic reaction can make all the difference.

☛ **DON'T** force victim to lie down. Whatever makes for easier breathing is good.

UNCONSCIOUSNESS

A victim seems to be sleeping, but can't be woken up.

WHAT TO LOOK FOR

- Sleeping victim who won't wake up
- Flushed, white, or blue face and gums

WHAT YOU SHOULD DO

1. Get medical help right away. Call 911 or operator (0) or EMS

Until you get help:

2. Check breathing. If breathing stops, use assist breathing. (See page 10.)

3. If the neck or back is hurt, don't move victim.

   a. If neck or back isn't hurt, lay victim down.

4. Loosen clothing.

5. Turn victim onto side to prevent choking in case of vomiting.

WHAT YOU SHOULD NOT DO

- ☛ **DON'T** give victim anything to eat or drink.
- ☛ **DON'T** leave victim alone.
- ☛ **DON'T** move victim if you think their head, neck or back may be injured.

FAINTING

Temporary unconsciousness

Fainting

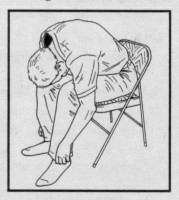

WHAT TO LOOK FOR

- Weak and dizzy
- Cold perspiration
- Rapid and weak pulse
- Shallow breathing

WHAT YOU SHOULD DO

1. If the victim feels faint, or is about to faint, let him/her sit down, head between the knees.

2. If the person faints, make him/her lie down with head lower than the feet.

3. If the victim remains unconscious, call 911 or operator (0) or EMS.

Until help comes:

4. Treat the victim for shock. (See page 38.)

5. Make sure victim can breathe. (See page 10.)

WHAT YOU SHOULD NOT DO

- ☛ **DON'T** give anything to drink.

POISONING

WHAT TO LOOK FOR
- Bloody vomit
- Burns or stains on lips, mouth, and tongue
- Cramps, nausea, or vomiting
- Overexcitement
- Rapid breathing
- Ringing in the ears
- Stomach or throat pain or burning sensation
- Strange odor on breath
- Unconsciousness
- Drowsiness

Poisoning

WHAT YOU SHOULD DO

Follow instructions from emergency personnel over phone.

1. Get emergency help right away. Call 911, operator (0), EMS or 1-800-222-1222 (Poison Control Center).

2. Look around for container with poison.

3. Have container of poison ready when you call. Read label on container to emergency personnel. Tell them how much was swallowed and when.

   a. Give container to EMS when they arrive.

4. Follow instructions from emergency personnel over phone.

Until help comes:

5. Don't give antidotes or induce vomiting unless emergency personnel tell you to.

6. If victim throws up, be sure his/her head is turned to side. Clean out mouth afterward.

If victim is convulsing (throwing arms and legs around):

7. Check breathing.

   a. Give assist breathing. (See page 10.)

8. Loosen tight clothing.

WHAT YOU SHOULD <u>NOT</u> DO
☛ **DON'T** make victim throw up:
   a. If the victim has swallowed a strong acid, alkali or petroleum product
   b. If the victim is unconscious or semiconscious
   c. If the victim is convulsing
   d. If the victim has a serious heart problem
☛ **DON'T** give anything by mouth unless emergency personnel tell you to.
☛ **DON'T** restrain victim having convulsions.

BITES

WHAT TO LOOK FOR
- Teeth marks on skin
- Skin may be open and bleeding

Don't apply a tourniquet.

WHAT YOU SHOULD DO
1. Get medical help right away. Call 911 or operator (0) or EMS.

Until you get help:

2. Control bleeding by direct pressure and raising bitten arm or leg. (See page 16.)

   a. If the wound is a puncture without heavy bleeding, wash it with soap and water. Rinse for 10 minutes.

   b. Put a sterile (germ-free) dressing or a clean cloth over wound and hold it in place with a bandage.

   c. If bleeding is heavy, don't remove original dressing. Just secure it in place with a bandage.

3. Check bitten victim for signs of shock. (See page 38.)

WHAT YOU SHOULD NOT DO
☞ **DON'T** try to clean wound if it's bleeding heavily.
☞ **DON'T** apply a tourniquet.
☞ **DON'T** give alcohol or aspirin.
☞ **DON'T** try to catch animal yourself. Call your local animal warden or the police.

Wash animal bites

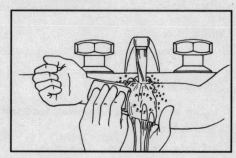

Direct pressure to stop bleeding

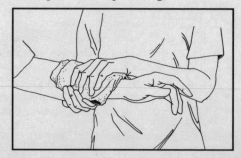

SNAKEBITE

There are different symptoms for different snakebites.

WHAT TO LOOK FOR

- A sharp, stinging pain around bite
- Puncture marks
- Swelling, puffiness, discoloration
- Weakness
- No feeling in bitten arm or leg
- Nausea and vomiting
- Weak and rapid pulse
- Hard to breathe
- Blurred vision
- Sweating
- Drooling
- Mumbling or slurred speech
- Delirium (confusion)

Don't suck the venom from the wound.

WHAT YOU SHOULD DO

1. Get medical help right away. Call 911 or operator (0) or EMS.

Until help arrives:

2. Keep the victim lying down and quiet with the injured part not moving and lower than the rest of the body.

    a. If bite is on neck or head, lay victim with head lower than the heart.

3. Remove all jewelry from the arm.

4. Wash bite.

    a. Pat dry with clean cloth.

5. Lightly press down with a gauze wrap or roller bandage on the arm or leg above the wound.

6. Keep the arm or leg from moving.

7. Treat for shock.

8. Identify the snake if you can.

WHAT YOU SHOULD <u>NOT</u> DO

- ☞ **DON'T** suck the venom from the wound with your mouth.
- ☞ **DON'T** give the victim anything by mouth.
- ☞ **DON'T** cut into the bite.
- ☞ **DON'T** squeeze bite.
- ☞ **DON'T** apply a tourniquet.
- ☞ **DON'T** place ice on the bite.
- ☞ **DON'T** let victim walk.
- ☞ **DON'T** try to capture snake.

INSECT STING

WHAT TO LOOK FOR
- Pain, Burning or Itching
- Swelling or Puffiness
- Redness

WHAT YOU SHOULD DO
1. If there are allergic reaction signs (swelling of the tongue and face, difficulty in breathing), see Allergic Reaction, page 39.

2. If there is no sign of allergic reaction remove stinger from skin. Don't squeeze stinger.

3. Wash stung area with soap and water. Be gentle.

4. Apply an ice bag or ice in a towel to area.

WHAT YOU SHOULD <u>NOT</u> DO
☛ **DON'T** squeeze stinger or use tweezers to remove stinger

BITES AND STINGS OF SPIDERS, CENTIPEDES AND SCORPIONS

WHAT TO LOOK FOR
- Small skin punctures
- Puffiness or swelling
- Redness
- Burning pain
- Sweating
- Tiredness
- Nausea
- Cramps in the back, shoulders, chest, arms and legs
- Fever
- Blood in urine

Don't try to suck the venom from spider bites with your mouth.

WHAT YOU SHOULD DO
1. Get medical help right away. Call 911 or operator (0) or EMS.

Until help comes:

2. Put a cold pack on the area. You can use frozen peas in a bag. Wrap in towel.

3. Keep the victim quiet.

4. If the bite is on an arm or leg, splint it.

WHAT YOU SHOULD <u>NOT</u> DO
☛ **DON'T** try to suck the venom from spider bites.

POISON IVY, POISON OAK AND POISON SUMAC

WHAT TO LOOK FOR
- Itching and burning
- Red rash
- Blisters
- Swelling, puffiness

Don't burn clothing that's been in contact with plants.

WHAT YOU SHOULD DO
1. Take off clothing that may have touched plants.

2. Wash the body area that touched the plant with soap and water.

3. Wash yourself as well.

4. See a doctor if blisters or bad rash develops.

WHAT YOU SHOULD NOT DO
☛ **DON'T** burn clothing that's been in contact with plants

FROSTBITE

Extreme cold can freeze unprotected parts of the body.

WHAT TO LOOK FOR

- Waxy, white or yellowish-gray areas of skin
- Burning or itching sensations
- Reddened and swollen skin
- Skin hard or frozen to the touch
- Blotchy skin
- Blisters
- Pain
- Numbness

WHAT YOU SHOULD DO

1. Get medical help right away. Call 911 or operator (0) or EMS.

Until help comes:

2. Warm frostbitten parts by placing them against victim's body or your own body.

3. Take victim indoors or out of the cold.

4. Dip frostbitten body part in lukewarm — not hot — water. If you don't have lukewarm water, cover with blankets or warm towels.

5. Take the arm or leg out of water or take off coverings once skin becomes warm.

6. Raise frostbitten arms or legs to start blood circulating.

7. Separate frostbitten toes and fingers with clean cloth.

8. Gently dry frostbitten area.

WHAT YOU SHOULD __NOT__ DO

- ☛ **DON'T** rub or massage frostbitten parts.
- ☛ **DON'T** rewarm area with hot water or high heat from open flame.
- ☛ **DON'T** allow victim to walk on frostbitten feet.
- ☛ **DON'T** break blisters.
- ☛ **DON'T** use hot water bottles or heat lamps.
- ☛ **DON'T** let victim smoke.
- ☛ **DON'T** let the victim drink coffee, tea or hot chocolate

Don't rub or massage frostbitten area.

Frostbite

HEATSTROKE (Sunstroke)

The body becomes overheated.

WHAT TO LOOK FOR

- Sudden fever, high body temperature (higher than 106 °F.)
- Red, hot, dry skin
- No perspiration
- Elevated pulse rate
- Fainting
- Possible confusion
- Vomiting
- Diarrhea
- Seizures

Put victim in cool bath.

WHAT YOU SHOULD DO

1. Get medical help right away. Call 911 or operator (0) or EMS.

Until help comes:

2. Undress victim.

3. Wrap in cool, wet towels.

4. Place ice packs wrapped in towels or cloth at neck, armpits and groin.

5. Put in cool bath.

6. Spray with cold water from a hose.

7. Keep cooling until temperature has dropped to 102 degrees. Don't overcool. Keep taking victim's temperature.

Heatstroke

8. Once temperature has been lowered, dry victim off.

9. Place in front of fan or in an air-conditioned room.

10. Watch for shock. (See page 38.)

11. Check breathing. If it stops, use assist breathing. (See page 10.)

WHAT YOU SHOULD **NOT** DO

☞ **DON'T** give any alcohol.

SPRAINS, STRAINS, FRACTURES AND DISLOCATIONS

Sprains are injuries caused when a ligament holding a joint together has been stretched or torn. A strain is an injury caused by pulling or overexerting a muscle. If you don't know whether the injury is a sprain or strain, treat it as a fracture.

WHAT TO LOOK FOR

- Pain on movement
- Tenderness
- Swelling, puffiness
- Discoloration

WHAT YOU SHOULD DO

1. Place the victim in a comfortable position.

2. Raise the injured area and don't use it.

3. For the first 24 hours, put an ice bag wrapped in a towel over the sprained area for 30 minutes, then off for 30 minutes.

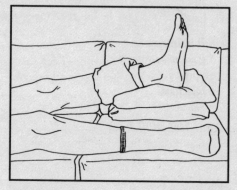

Reduce swelling of sprain

4. If pain or swelling is severe, and to be sure it's not a bone fracture, see a doctor.

FRACTURES AND DISLOCATIONS

A fracture is any bone that has been broken or cracked. A dislocation is an injury to a joint and the ligaments around the joint.

- Open (compound) fracture. The bone is broken and there's an open wound. The broken bone may protrude from the wound.
- Closed (simple) fracture. No open wound is present, but there is a broken or cracked bone.
- Give the same emergency first aid for both fractures and dislocations.
- If fracture is serious, don't try to put on a splint.

WHAT TO LOOK FOR

- Bone sticking out from the skin
- Bone or joint looks crooked or strange
- Grinding sensation during movement
- Pain, tenderness
- Hard to move
- Swelling, puffiness, discoloration

WHAT YOU SHOULD DO

1. Get medical help right away.
   Call 911 or operator (0) or EMS.

2. Assume back or neck injury if victim is unconscious or has head injury, neck pain or tingling in arms and leg. Don't move victim if you think their neck, back or head may be injured. (See pages 21 and 24.)

If fracture is serious, don't try to put on a splint.

Until help comes:

3. Keep bones from moving. Keep them in the same position you found them. (See below.)

4. Use direct pressure to control bleeding. Don't raise the injured area. (See page 17.)

5. If bone is protruding (sticking out from the skin), cover with gauze or clean cloth once bleeding has been stopped.

6. Check for shock. (See page 38.)

   a. If there's no open wound, put on an ice pack wrapped in towel or clean cloth.

WHAT YOU SHOULD **NOT** DO

☛ **NO** food or drink.

☛ **DON'T** let victim move affected area.

☛ **DON'T** move victim if you think head, neck or back may be injured.

☛ **DON'T** try to push back any bone that's sticking out.

☛ **DON'T** move victim with suspected head, back or neck injury. Wait for emergency crew.

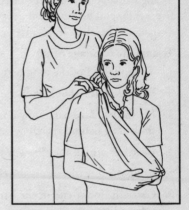

Keep broken bones from moving

STOP BROKEN BONES FROM MOVING *(IMMOBILIZING FRACTURES)*

Use a splint to stop broken bones from moving. You can make a splint from a board, a broom handle or even a rolled-up magazine or newspaper.

When you have to splint a broken bone, do this:

1. Gently remove all clothing from any suspected fracture or dislocation.

2. Don't try to push bones back through an open wound.

3. Don't try to straighten any fracture.

4. Cover open wounds with a sterile dressing before splinting.

49

5. Pad splints with soft material.

6. Pad under all natural arches of the body such as the knee and wrist.

7. Support the injured part while splint is being applied.

8. Splint firmly, but not tightly.

9. Elevate the injured part and use ice (not directly on the skin — wrap ice in a towel) or a cold compress when you can.

A sling is like a hammock for the arm. Use it for injuries to the shoulder, arms or ribs. Make a sling from triangular or cravat bandages. Or make a sling from a belt, necktie or scarf.

Triangular bandages are large three-sided pieces of cloth. The long side is about five feet long. The other two sides are each about three feet long. You can make a triangular bandage from a clean bedsheet.

Triangular Bandage Sling

1. Take one end of the long part (the base) of an open triangular bandage.

2. Put it over the shoulder of the injured side.

3. Let the bandage hang down in front of the chest. That way the pointed tip will be behind the elbow of the injured arm.

4. Bend the arm at the elbow with hand slightly raised four to five inches.

5. Bring the forearm across the chest and over the bandage.

6. Carry the lower end of the bandage over the shoulder on the uninjured side and tie on uninjured side of the neck (toward the back).

7. Twist the pointed tip of the bandage, and tuck it in at the elbow.

Cravat Bandage Sling

To make a cravat bandage, fold a triangular bandage into a strip.

1. Spread the triangular bandage out. The long side should be closest to you. The point should be on top.

2. Take that top point and fold it toward you until it touches the longest side (the "base").

3. Then fold the bandage in half again, and you have a cravat bandage. It will be long and skinny.

4. Place one end over the shoulder of the injured side.

5. Let the bandage hang down in front of the chest.

6. Bend the arm at the elbow with hand slightly raised 4 to 5 inches.

7. Bring the forearm across the chest and over the bandage.

8. Carry the lower end of the bandage over the injured arm to the shoulder on the uninjured side and tie at uninjured side of neck (toward the back).

PUTTING SLINGS AND SPLINTS TO USE

Shoulder And Collarbone

WHAT YOU SHOULD DO

1 Place victim's forearm at right angle across chest, with hand raised above elbow level.

2. Apply sling. Tie sling at back of neck.

3. Bind arm to victim's body by placing towel or cloth over sling and around upper arm and chest. Tie under the opposite arm.

4. Keep checking fingers. If they turn numb, cold, blue or swell (get puffy), loosen towel or cloth.

Broken collarbone

Bent Elbow

WHAT YOU SHOULD DO

1. Don't try to straighten elbow.

2. Splint arm in the position found in.

   a. Pad splint. Wrap it in cloth, towels or blanket.

   b. Bind splint to arm above and below elbow using anything like neckties, scarves or belts.

3. Place forearm in sling. Raise the hand above the elbow level. Tie the sling at back of neck.

4. Bind arm to victim's body by placing towel or cloth over sling and around upper arm and chest. Tie under opposite arm.

5. Keep checking fingers. If they turn numb, cold, blue or swell (get puffy), loosen the binding.

Broken elbow

Straight Elbow

WHAT YOU SHOULD DO

1. Don't bend elbow.

2. Apply a padded splint from armpit to hand.

    a. Pad splint with cloth, towels or blanket.

    b. Bind splint to arm above and below elbow using anything like neckties, scarves or belts.

3. Keep checking fingers. If they turn numb, cold, blue or swell (get puffy), loosen the binding.

Arm, Wrist And Hand

WHAT YOU SHOULD DO

Arm fractures

1. Place padded splint under lower arm and hand.

    a. Bind splint to arm using neckties, cloth or belts. Don't bind directly over break.

2. Keep checking fingers. If they turn numb, cold, blue or swell (get puffy), loosen binding.

3. Place splinted arm in sling. Hand should be above elbow level.

4. Keep arms from moving. Bind it to victim's body by wrapping towel or cloth over sling and around upper arm and chest. Tie towel or cloth under the other arm.

Knee

WHAT YOU SHOULD DO

1. Splint knee in position found. If knee is straight, place a long, padded splint, extended from heel to buttocks, under victim's leg. Cushion knee and ankle with extra padding. If knee is bent, place splint on side of leg.

    a. Tie splint around the leg at ankle, thigh and lower leg. Don't tie over kneecap.

2. Keep checking toes. If they turn numb, cold, blue or swell (get puffy), loosen binding.

Leg And Ankle

WHAT YOU SHOULD DO

1. Keep leg and ankle from moving with padded splints placed on sides of leg. Make sure the splints extend from below heel to above knee.

   a. Tie splints together using neckties, belts, cloth or rope. Don't tie directly over break.

2. If you don't have a splint, place a folded blanket between legs. Tie legs together. Don't tie directly over break.

3. Keep checking toes. If they turn numb, cold, blue or swell (get puffy), loosen binding

Don't let toes or fingers turn numb, cold, blue or swell (get puffy).

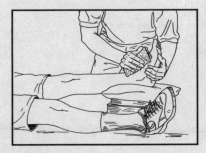

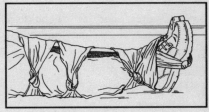

Broken leg

Foot And Toe

WHAT YOU SHOULD DO

1. Remove shoe.

2. Wrap folded up towels, a blanket or a pillow around foot as a splint. Don't bend foot or toe.

3. Tie padding around foot.

4. Keep checking unbroken toes for signs of tight binding. If they turn numb, cold, blue or swell (get puffy), loosen binding.

WHAT YOU SHOULD NOT DO

☛ **DON'T** let toes or fingers turn numb, cold, blue or swell (get puffy).

ILLNESSES & MEDICAL EMERGENCIES

Medical emergencies include certain disorders and conditions.

DIABETIC EMERGENCIES

WHAT TO LOOK FOR
Diabetic Coma
- Warm and dry skin
- Sunken eyes
- Rapid and labored breathing
- Rapid and weak pulse
- Excessive urination
- Extreme thirst
- Nausea and vomiting
- Abdominal pain
- Sickly sweet odor (like nail polish remover) on the breath
- Confusion, resembling drunkenness

Don't give an unconscious person anything to eat or drink.

WHAT TO LOOK FOR
Insulin Shock
- Hunger
- Confusion
- Headache
- Sweating a lot
- Rapid, weak pulse
- Dizziness
- Fast breathing
- Finally convulsions and unconsciousness

WHAT YOU SHOULD DO
1. Call 911 or operator (0) or EMS.

2. Watch for vomiting.

3. Maintain an open airway.

4. Treat the victim for shock.

WHAT YOU SHOULD NOT DO
☛ **DON'T** give an unconscious person anything to eat or drink.

EPILEPTIC SEIZURES

Grand mal and petit mal are the seizures which may occur. Of these two, grand mal is more severe.

WHAT TO LOOK FOR
Petit mal
- Only partial loss of consciousness, if any, occurs.
- The victim remains aware of things around him.
- Jerky movements of the eyes or arms and legs.

WHAT TO LOOK FOR
Grand mal
- The victim may feel an attack coming.
- Loss of consciousness.
- Body becomes rigid, then convulsed.
- There may be loss of bowel and bladder control.
- The face gets pale and then turns blue.
- Teeth may bite down on tongue.
- Breathing may be loud and noisy.
- The victim may froth at the mouth.
- The seizure only lasts for a few minutes.
- After the seizure the victim may be very tired and sleepy.

Keep the victim calm.

WHAT YOU SHOULD DO
1. Keep the victim calm.

2. Don't restrain the victim.

3. Protect the victim from injury by removing anything that he could bump into.

4. When the seizure is over:

   a. Keep his airway open.

   b. Allow the victim to rest.

WHAT YOU SHOULD NOT DO
☛ **DON'T** give him anything to eat or drink during the seizure.
☛ **DON'T** put any objects in the mouth, including your fingers.

HEART ATTACK

WHAT TO LOOK FOR

- Uncomfortable pressure, squeezing, fullness or dull pain in the chest or upper abdomen ("indigestion")
- Pain into the shoulders, arms, neck or jaws
- Difficulty breathing (shortness of breath)
- Rapid heart rate
- Sweating with nausea or vomiting
- Weak
- Pale

Keep the victim at rest and in a comfortable position.

WHAT YOU SHOULD DO

1. Call 911 or operator (0) or EMS.

2. Keep the victim at rest and in a comfortable position.

3. Loosen tight clothing.

4. Cover the victim to prevent chill, but don't warm the victim.

5. Reassure the victim.

6. Check with your doctor first to make sure there are no contraindications, in which case aspirin may be helpful.

WHAT YOU SHOULD <u>NOT</u> DO

- ☞ **DON'T** make victim lie down flat.
- ☞ **DON'T** give any food or drink.

Heart attack

STROKE

WHAT TO LOOK FOR
- Confusion, memory lapse or loss
- Impaired speech
- Paralysis or weakness on one side of the body or face
- Abnormal pupil size or gaze
- Difficulty breathing
- Slurred speech
- Unconsciousness

WHAT YOU SHOULD DO

Keep the victim quiet and calm.

1. Call 911 or operator (0) or EMS.
2. Maintain an open airway.

   a. Keep the tongue or saliva from blocking the air passage.

3. Keep the conscious victim lying down.

   a. Keep the head and shoulders raised (semi-sitting position).

5. Keep the victim quiet and calm.

WHAT YOU SHOULD <u>NOT</u> DO
☞ **DON'T** give the victim anything by mouth.
☞ **DON'T** move the victim any more than necessary.

LABOR (Emergency Childbirth)

WHAT TO LOOK FOR
- Contractions less than 2 minutes apart

WHAT YOU SHOULD DO

Remain calm and reassure the mother.

Call 911 or operator (0) or EMS.

Until help comes:

1. Remain calm and reassure the mother.
2. Follow the instructions on the phone.

WHAT YOU SHOULD <u>NOT</u> DO
☞ **DON'T** try to delay childbirth.

2 KID STUFF

SUDDEN ILLNESS

CROUP COUGH

Child has a cough at night that sounds like a dog barking.

WHAT TO LOOK FOR
- Barking or hacking cough
- Wheezing or whistling breathing noise
- Hoarseness
- Trouble breathing

WHAT YOU SHOULD DO

1. If child has trouble breathing, makes a croaking sound when breathing in or turns blue, call 911 or operator (0) or EMS.

Until help comes:

2. Sit with your child in a steamy bathroom for 15 minutes. Fill the bathroom with steam by running the hot water for a few minutes while the bathroom door is closed.

   a. Don't put the child in the tub.

   b. Read a story to him.

WHAT YOU SHOULD NOT DO
- ☛ **DON'T** put anything in the child's mouth.
- ☛ **DON'T** give child any cough medicine.

Don't put anything in the child's mouth.

CHOKING

Something may be blocking your child's airway.

WHAT TO LOOK FOR
- A lot of coughing
- Child doesn't speak or cry
- Child passes out

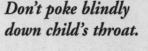

*Don't poke blindly
down child's throat.*

WHAT YOU SHOULD DO

1. If child is coughing, there is no need to do anything, but stay close by him.

2. If child tries to cough but can't, or is having trouble breathing, or passes out, call 911 or operator (0) or EMS.

Until help comes:

For baby younger than 1 year old:

1. Hold baby face down across your forearm.

2. Hold the baby's jaw to support his head. Keep head lower than chest.

3. Firmly hit the upper part of his back between the shoulder blades five times with the heel of your hand.

4. Repeat until whatever is choking your baby pops out. Take it out of baby's mouth.

5. If nothing came out, turn your baby over on your lap or thigh.

6. Keep baby's head lower than its chest.

7. Place your three middle fingers on the middle of baby's chest.

8. Push down five times until whatever's choking your baby pops out.

*Assist breathing for
babies*

9. Push down sharply once every second.

10. If it doesn't pop out, look in his mouth to see if there's anything there. Use a finger to take it out.

11. If the thing still hasn't popped out, repeat steps 3 to 10.

12. If baby is still not breathing, begin mouth-to-nose rescue breathing:

    a. Remove anything blocking baby's mouth.

    b. Put your lips around both baby's mouth and nose and breath into his lungs

    c. Make sure your lips are making a really tight leak-proof seal.

    d. Blow gently five times into lungs.

    e. Check for breathing, coughing or swallowing.

13. Repeat until help comes or baby starts breathing.

For child older than 1 year who is sitting up or standing, but can't cough or speak, call 911 or operator (0) or EMS.

Until help comes:

1. Stand behind child. Perform the Heimlich maneuver.

2. Wrap your hands around child's waist, over the hips.

3. Make a fist with one hand.

4. Put the thumb side of your fist on child's abdomen, the upper stomach, right below the ribs, just above the navel. Don't touch the breastbone.

5. Put your other hand over your fist.

6. Press sharply upward into child's stomach five times.

7. Keep doing this until whatever is choking your child pops out.

8. If it doesn't pop out, use a finger to take out anything you see inside the mouth.

9. If child goes limp, start assist breathing. (See page 10.)

For child older than one year who is lying unconscious, call 911 or operator (0) or EMS.

Until help comes:

1. Turn child so that he is facing up.

2. Put the heel of one hand on your child's upper stomach, right under the ribs.

3. Put your other hand on top of your fist.

4. Push your fist quickly into your child's stomach.

5. Keep doing this until the thing choking your child pops out.

6. If it doesn't pop out, start assist breathing. (See page 10.)

WHAT YOU SHOULD <u>NOT</u> DO

☛ **DON'T** give your child anything to drink.

☛ **DON'T** shake baby.

☛ **DON'T** use abdominal (stomach) thrusts on a baby younger than one year old.

☛ **DON'T** stick your finger blindly down baby's throat to poke around.

Heimlich maneuver for child

FEVER CONVULSIONS

High fevers need special attention. They can sometimes lead to convulsions or seizures.

WHAT TO LOOK FOR

- Temperatures of 100.2° F or higher when the baby is 3 months or younger
- Baby has a temperature of 101° F or higher when 3 to 6 months old
- Baby older than 6 months has a temperature of 103° F or higher
- Headache
- Stiff neck   ***Don't give aspirin to children.***
- Throat swells up
- Purple spots on the skin
- Convulsions (arms or legs twitch, fists may clench, back may get stiff)

WHAT YOU SHOULD DO

1. If your child has a fever seizure, call your doctor. If your child is having trouble breathing, call 911 or operator (0) or EMS.

2. Take off your child's clothes down to underwear.

3. Put your child to bed to rest.

4. Dip a cloth or towel into cold water and put it on your child's forehead and neck.

5. Sponge your child with water that is lukewarm.

6. If your child starts to shiver, stop the sponging and cover your child with a light blanket.

WHAT YOU SHOULD <u>NOT</u> DO

- ☛ **DON'T** try to stop arms and legs from twitching.
- ☛ **DON'T** put your child in a tub.
- ☛ **DON'T** put anything in your child's mouth during a seizure.
- ☛ **DON'T** give aspirin to children.

Fever convulsion

CUTS, BUMPS, BITES AND BRUISES

How To Handle Minor Complaints

Call your doctor if you see signs of infection (red streaks leading from wound), pain, swelling (puffiness), pus or warmth, or if child runs a fever or complains about pain. In an emergency, call 911 or operator (0) or EMS.

Blisters. Let small blisters heal on their own. If blister is broken, wash raw skin with soap and water and cover with a bandage. Important: If the blister is large, or if there's redness, puffiness, pus or pain, bring child to a doctor.

Bruises. Wring out a towel in cold water and put it on the hurt part for a half hour.

Cramp. A pain in the foot or lower leg (calf) can be relieved by stretching and massage. While your child is sitting, raise his leg and straighten knee. Gently push toes upward and forward. Gently work your fingertips (knead and squeeze) into the calf muscle until the cramp disappears.

Earwax. If wax gets hard, put a few drops of warm baby oil in your child's ear twice a day for 5 days. Don't do this if your child has any other ear problems. Never put Q-tips or any other object in child's ears.

Heat Rash. Sponge down your undressed child with cool water. After his skin has almost dried, put on some calamine lotion or cream. Bathe a baby in tepid water and pat almost dry, leaving skin a little damp.

Hiccups. Have the child breathe in and out of a paper bag for a minute or two. If hiccups go on and on, see a doctor.

Lump or Bump. Put an ice pack on the spot. Don't put ice directly on the area. Wrap the ice in a towel. You can also use a bag of frozen peas wrapped in a towel. If the head has been injured, see a doctor. Also see a doctor if a lump, bump or bruise anywhere on the body is large or very painful.

Scrape. Always wash your hands with soap and water before treating any injury. After washing your hands, wash your child's injured spot with soap and water. Don't scrub hard. Don't put any medication on the scrape. You don't have to cover scrapes if they are small. Big scratches should be covered, though. Place a small gauze pad on wound and tape it down. Keep an eye on the scrape. If it gets red, painful or puffs up, see a doctor immediately or call 911 or operator (0) or EMS.

Scratch. Control bleeding if it is a deep scratch. Always wash your hands with soap and water before treating any injury. After washing your hands, wash your child's injured spot with soap and water. Don't scrub hard. Control bleeding by pressing down with a clean gauze pad. After stopping bleeding, place a small gauze pad on wound and tape it down. Keep an eye on the scratch. If it gets red, painful or puffs up, see a doctor immediately or call 911 or operator (0) or EMS.

Always wash your hands with soap and water before treating any injury.

Control bleeding (child)

Stye. (inflamed eyelid) If the eyelid is tender, put a warm, damp cloth or hand towel on it. Don't squeeze the stye. If it comes back or doesn't go away in a day or two, see a doctor.

Sunburn. If skin gets blistered, give child cool baths and put a cool wet towel on the sunburn. Don't use any ointments, sprays or butter.

Tick Bites. Remove tick with tweezers, never your fingers. Pull the tick out slowly and steadily. Clean where the tick bit with rubbing alcohol. Wash your own hands. Flush tick down the toilet. Tell your doctor about the tick bite.

SWALLOWING THE WRONG THING

Your child can get sick from many different things. It's important to act quickly if you think your child may have put something dangerous in his mouth.

WHAT TO LOOK FOR

- Strange smell on child's breath
- Stains or burns around child's mouth
- Child is sleepy before regular naptime
- Eyes go around in circles
- Opened or spilled bottle of pills

Even after poison-proofing your home, prepare for emergencies.

WHAT YOU SHOULD DO

1. Call 911 or operator (0) or EMS or Poison Control Center (1-800-222-1222).

2. Give them this information:

   a. Your child's age, height and weight

   b. Any medical problems and general health of the child

   c. What poison was taken if you know

   d. How was it taken (swallowed? chewed? splashed in the eyes? Breathed in?)

   e. Whether child has vomited.

3. If you know what poison was taken, bring the bottle with you to the phone and read the label to the emergency professional.

4. Follow the directions of the emergency personnel or poison control center exactly.

5. Remain calm.

WHAT YOU SHOULD NOT DO

☛ **DON'T** give any at-home antidote or medicine before checking with emergency professionals.

Prevent Childhood Poisoning

- Always close any container holding medicine as soon as you've finished using it.
- Never bring any medication or pills into the house that doesn't have child-resistant packaging.
- Make sure the child-resistant packaging is good and tight.
- Put the medicine away immediately in a place where children can't reach it.
- Keep all medications and pills in their original containers.
- Never carry pills loose.
- Keep all medicines out of reach and out of sight of children.
- Never keep medicines on a countertop or bedside table.
- Follow medicine label directions carefully.
- Buy only as much as you need of such hazardous products such as paint

thinners or nail polish remover.
- Never tell a child that some medicine he may have to take is candy.
- Teach kids to stay away from cleaning products.
- Never put these substances into other containers.
- Lock any cabinet containing an item that may be poisonous.
- Use locked cabinets in garages and utility rooms for antifreeze, windshield-washing fluid and other hazardous products.
- Use childproof cabinet latches.
- Make sure all plants around your house are kid-safe and pet-safe. Dangerous plants include such old favorites as rhododendron and holly.
- Keep the medicines of any visitors away from children.
- Don't chuck old medications in the wastebasket. Throw them out with the trash.
- Keep children and pets away while applying pesticides, indoors or outdoors.

Lock poisons away

- Don't leave a pesticide package open if you haven't finished using it.
- Talk to your kids about the danger of putting things in their mouths.
- Kids can be poisoned by many seemingly innocent things, including plants, lipstick and cough medicine. Stay aware.

Even after poison-proofing your home, prepare for emergencies.
- Place the numbers of the poison control center and your doctor by your phone.
- Add syrup of ipecac and activated charcoal to your first-aid kit. (These should only be used when you're told to do so by emergency professionals.)

Lead
Your children can be poisoned if they get lead in their bodies.
- Have your children tested for lead. This test is often free at local health clinics.
- Find out if your home, soil or water has lead. Your local or state health department can tell you how to do this with little or no cost.
- Only trained workers should remove lead.
- Protect your children from lead. Wash their hands and face often with soap and water, especially before they eat. Wash toys every week.
- Never sweep, vacuum or dry dust in a room that has lead dust.
- Don't let children chew on, or put their mouths on window sills.
- Keep cribs away from window sills and walls.
- Never dry scrape or dry sand lead paint. Don't try to burn it or torch it.
- Never use hot water from the tap for drinking, cooking or making formula.
- Let the cold water run for a few minutes before using it.

CALMING A FRIGHTENED CHILD

If there's a fire in your home, if somebody gets really sick, or you're in an accident, your child will look to you for help and answers.

Here's what you should do:

Hug your children.

- Be calm and reassuring. If you're relaxed, your child will also be relaxed.
- Be cheerful, even about things like sores and stings. It's the way to steer clear of fears and tears.
- Don't let your feelings get the best of you. Don't start crying yourself. You have to be brave for your child's sake. Tell your child, "That's really nothing. It'll go away. You'll soon feel better."

What you should say to and do for a child when something bad is happening or has happened:

1. Touch your child. Hug him or her for reassurance.

2. Get down and talk to your child. Don't stand above him.

3. Don't lose your temper or get annoyed. Kids can't explain things clearly sometimes, like when they're frightened or they don't feel well. Be patient when they try to tell you they have an ache and they can't tell you where or what it is.

4. Be clear and simple in your instructions and what you're doing. "Now I'm going to put this bandage on you." Or "Help me by holding your hand this way. That's right!"

BONUS: Being quiet and confident when talking to your child will also calm you down!

After an emergency or disaster, like a fire, accident or sickness in the family, children are going to be afraid that:

1. The event will happen again.

2. They will be separated from the family.

3. They will be left alone.

Adults can make emergencies and disasters less upsetting for children. Here's what you can do:

1. The best help you can give a child is to be calm, honest and caring.

2. Listen to what the child is saying.

   a. If a young child asks questions about the event, Don't ignore them. Don't be abrupt or impatient. Answer them simply and sincerely.

b. If a child can't put into words his feelings, let him draw you a picture or tell a story of what has happened.

3. Hug and touch your children.

4. Calmly and gently tell the truth about what just happened.

5. Encourage your children to talk about their feelings. Be honest about your own feelings, but also be reassuring and upbeat.

6. Spend extra time with your children at bedtime.

7. As soon as you can, start a schedule for work, play, meals and rest. Children like routine and rules in their lives.

8. Give your children specific chores to help them feel they are an important part of the family and that they're helping to make things all right.

9. Praise and recognize sensible and "grown-up" behavior.

3 DISASTER CONDITIONS

FAMILY DISASTER PLAN

Prepare for a disaster before it happens. Your family will then be better able to handle the emergency, even if help is slow getting to you.

Plan and think safety by preparing for tomorrow.

- Obtain hazard specific homeowners insurance to cover your contents and structure or renters insurance to cover your contents.
- Maintain a battery operated radio and a NOAA Weather Radio.
- Prepare a family disaster supplies kit and keep it current and handy.
- Develop a family evacuation plan and practice it once a year.
- Pay attention to all emergency warnings — follow directions and evacuate your residence when advised to do so.

Plan how your family will stay in contact if separated.

Pick two meeting places:

1. A location a safe distance from your home in case of fire.

2. A place outside your neighborhood or immediate area in case you can't return home. Arrange for an out-of-state friend to be a "check-in-contact" for everyone to call.

Do all this now.

Smoke alarms

- Post emergency telephone numbers by every phone in the house and on the refrigerator door, if you use it as the family bulletin board.
- Put emergency telephone numbers on all speed dialers, including cell phones.
- Post emergency telephone numbers on all your computers.
- Fill out and discuss the charts on the inside covers of this book.
- Show everyone how to and when to shut off water, gas and electricity at main switches.
- Install a smoke detector on each floor of your home, especially near bedrooms, but not in kitchen, where they'll be triggered every time you broil a hamburger. Test monthly and change the batteries twice a year, when you move clocks back or forward.

Think and Plan for Safety

Check outside and around your house, manufactured (mobile) home or apartment.

- Is it away from a river/creek or other water source that may flood?
- What fire department and ambulance service is available?
- How do you contact them in an emergency?
- Is the house near a fire hydrant?
- Are home entryways, parking areas and area streets well lit?
- Are the bushes and trees trimmed and away from roof, chimney, gutters and entryways?
- Are hallways and stairwells equipped with emergency lighting?
- Are play areas well-lit and free from hazards?
- If you have a pool, does it have a fence with a locked gate?

Check the inside of your house, manufactured (mobile) home or apartment.

- Are there smoke alarms installed on each level of the home and are they working?
- Are there fire extinguishers available and are they fully charged? (Your local fire department can tell you where to get them charged.)
- Are electrical outlets adequate and working? Don't overload outlets!
- Are the locks on windows and doors in working order?
- Are there at least two (2) ways to exit the residence?
- Are the chimney and gutters cleaned regularly?

FIRE

- Prepare your house, manufactured (mobile) home or apartment for fires.
- Check smoke alarms monthly and change the batteries at least once a year.
- If you must use a portable space heater, don't use near flammable objects such as curtains or furniture.

FLOODS

- Make sure the electric panel/fuse box is elevated above previous flood levels.
- Make sure the furnace, water heater, washer, dryer and other items in the basement are located off the floor and elevated above previous flood levels.

TORNADOES

- Go to a tornado safe room, if you have one, or to a room at the lowest level of your home, preferably in the center of the home (such as a bathroom or a closet).
- If you live in a mobile home park, be prepared to leave your home and go to a sturdy, well constructed building.

HURRICANES

- Have enough hurricane shutters or pre-cut plywood on hand to cover all windows and doors. Manufactured (mobile) homes, especially in areas where high winds occur, should be strapped or tied down to a foundation with cables or chains.

EARTHQUAKES

- Bolt tall furniture like bookcases and china cabinets to wall studs.
- Strap water heaters to wall studs.
- Install strong latches on cupboards. Have everyone in your home practice how to "drop, cover and hold on."

DISASTER SUPPLIES KIT

If a disaster happens, you are not going to have time to shop or search for supplies. That's why you should put together supplies now.

Look over the checklists.

Gather the supplies that are listed. Some supplies you will have on hand. You will have to shop for others. Do it soon, while you're thinking about it. You'll need them all if your family is unable to leave home. Certain supplies are marked with an asterisk (*). You'll need these if you have to leave the house in a hurry. Put these evacuation supplies in a container that's easy to carry.

You should stock six basics for your home:

(1) water, (2) food, (3) tools and emergency supplies, (4) clothing and bedding, (5) first-aid supplies and (6) special items.

1. Water

- Store water in plastic containers. Make sure the water storage container you plan to use is of food grade quality, such as 2-liter soda bottles, with tight-fitting screw-cap lids. Don't use milk cartons or glass bottles. These containers can decompose or break.
- Store one gallon (four quarts) of water per person in your family per day. A grownup needs to drink at least two quarts of water each day. Children, nursing mothers and sick people will need more.
- Keep at least a three-day supply of water per person (two quarts for drinking, two quarts for each person in your household for food preparation/sanitation).*
- If your local water is treated commercially by a water treatment utility, you don't have to treat the water before storing it. Check to find out.
- Change and replace stored water every six months.
- If you plan to use commercially prepared "spring" or "drinking" water, keep the water in its original sealed container.

2. Food

To judge how long you can store food supplies, look for an "expiration date" or "best if used by" date on the product. If you can not find a date on the product, then the general recommendation is to store food products for six months and then replace them.

- You will need enough supplies to last several days to a week.
- Avoid foods that are high in fat and protein.
- Don't stock salty foods, since they will make you thirsty.
- Stock canned foods that won't require cooking, water or special preparation.
- Store supplies of non-perishable foods and water in a handy place. You need to have these items packed and ready in case there is no time to gather food from the kitchen when disaster strikes.
- Foods that are compact and lightweight are easy to store and carry.
- Stock salt-free crackers, whole grain cereals and canned food with high liquid content.

Replace your stored food every six months.

Recommended foods include:

- Ready-to-eat canned meats, fruits and vegetables. (Be sure to include a manual can opener.)
- Canned juices, milk and soup (if powdered, store extra water).
- High energy foods, such as peanut butter, jelly, crackers, granola bars and trail mix.
- Comfort foods, such as hard candy, sweetened cereals, candy bars and cookies.
- Instant coffee, tea bags
- Foods for infants, elderly persons or persons on special diets, if necessary.
- Compressed food bars. They store well, are lightweight, taste good and are nutritious.
- Trail mix. It is available as a prepackaged product or you can assemble it on your own.
- Dried foods. They can be nutritious and satisfying, but some have a lot of salt content, which promotes thirst. Read the label.
- Freeze-dried foods. They are tasty and lightweight, but will need water for reconstitution.
- Instant Meals. Cups of noodles or cups of soup are a good addition, although they need water for reconstitution.
- Snack-sized canned goods. Good because they generally have pull-top lids or twist-open keys.
- Prepackaged beverages. Those in foil packets and foil-lined boxes are suitable because they are tightly sealed and will keep for a long time.

Avoid:

- Commercially dehydrated foods. They can require a great deal of water for reconstitution and extra effort in preparation.
- Bottled foods. They are generally too heavy and bulky, and break easily.
- Meal-sized canned foods. They are usually bulky and heavy.
- Whole grains, beans, pasta. Preparation could be complicated under the circumstances of a disaster.

3. Tools and Supplies

- Mess kits, or paper cups, plates and plastic utensils*
- *The Family Emergency Handbook**
- Battery-operated radio and extra batteries*
- Flashlight and extra batteries*
- Cash or traveler's checks, change*
- Non-electric can opener, utility knife*
- Fire extinguisher: small canister ABC type
- Tube tent
- Pliers
- Tape
- Compass
- Matches in a waterproof container
- Aluminum foil
- Plastic storage containers
- Signal flare
- Paper, pencil
- Needles, thread
- Medicine dropper
- Shut-off wrench, to turn off household gas and water
- Whistle
- Plastic sheeting
- Map of the area (for locating shelters)

Sanitation supplies

- Toilet paper, towelettes*
- Soap, liquid detergent*
- Feminine supplies*
- Personal hygiene items*
- Plastic garbage bags, ties (for personal sanitation uses)
- Plastic bucket with tight lid
- Disinfectant
- Household chlorine bleach

4. Clothing and Bedding

- Include at least one complete change of clothing and footwear per person.*

- Sturdy shoes or work boots*
- Rain gear*
- Blankets or sleeping bags*
- Hat and gloves
- Thermal underwear
- Sunglasses

5. First-Aid Kit

See page 5 for suggestions.

6. Special Items

Remember family members with special requirements, such as infants and elderly or disabled persons

Entertainment

- Games and books

Important Family Documents

For Baby*

- Formula
- Diapers
- Bottles
- Powdered milk
- Medications

For Adults*

- Heart and high blood pressure medication
- Insulin
- Prescription drugs
- Denture needs
- Contact lenses and supplies
- Extra eye glasses

Keep these records in a waterproof, portable container:
- Will, insurance policies, contracts, deeds, stocks and bonds
- Passports, social security cards, immunization records
- Bank account numbers
- Credit card account numbers and companies
- Inventory of valuable household goods, important telephone numbers
- Family records (birth, marriage, death certificates)

- Store your kit in a convenient place known to all family members. Keep a smaller version of the supplies kit in the trunk of your car.
- Keep items in airtight plastic bag
- Change your stored water supply every six months so it stays fresh.
- Replace your stored food every six months.
- Re-think your kit and family needs at least once a year. Replace batteries, update clothes, etc.
- Ask your physician or pharmacist about storing prescription medications.

*Keep items marked with an asterisk in an easy-to-carry container like a camping backpack. You would need these basics if you have to leave your home.

FIRE

WHAT TO DO BEFORE FIRE STRIKES

1. Install smoke alarms. Working smoke alarms decrease fatalities in a fire by half.

   - Place smoke alarms on every level of your home, outside bedrooms on the ceiling or high on the wall, at the top of open stairways or at the bottom of enclosed stairs and near (but not in) the kitchen.
   - Test and clean smoke alarms once a month and replace batteries at least once a year. Replace smoke alarms once every 10 years.

2. With your family, plan two escape routes from every room in the house. Practice with your household escaping from each room.

   - Make sure windows are not nailed or painted shut.
   - Make sure security gratings on windows have a fire safety-opening feature so that they can be easily opened from the inside.
   - Consider getting escape ladders if your home has more than one level.
   - Make sure that burglar bars and other antitheft mechanisms that block outside window entry can be easily opened from the inside.
   - Teach household members to stay low to the floor (where the air is safer in a fire) when escaping from a fire.
   - Pick a place outside your home for the household to meet after escaping from a fire.

3. Clean out storage areas. Don't let trash such as old newspapers and magazines accumulate.

4. Check the electrical wiring in your home:

   - Inspect extension cords for frayed or exposed wires or loose plugs.
   - Outlets should have cover plates and no exposed wiring.
   - Make sure wiring does not run under rugs, over nails or across high traffic areas.
   - Don't overload extension cords or outlets. If you need to plug in two or three appliances, get a UL-approved unit with built-in circuit breakers to prevent sparks and short circuits.

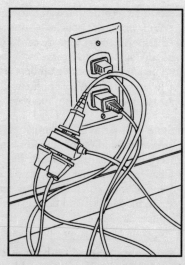

Fire Hazard

- Make sure home insulation does not touch electrical wiring.
- Have an electrician check the electrical wiring in your home.

5. Never use gasoline, benzine, naphtha or similar liquids indoors.

   - Store flammable liquids in approved containers in well-ventilated storage areas.
   - Never smoke near flammable liquids.
   - After use, safely discard all rags or materials soaked in flammable material.

6. Check chimneys, wood stoves and all home heating systems.

7. Insulate chimneys and place spark arresters on top.

8. Be careful when using wood, coal and kerosene heaters and electrical space heaters.

   - Place heaters at least three feet away from flammable materials.
   - Make sure the floor and nearby walls are properly insulated.
   - Use only the type of fuel designated for your unit and follow manufacturer's instructions.
   - Store ashes in a metal container outside and away from the residence.
   - Keep open flames away from walls, furniture, drapery and flammable items. Keep a screen in front of the fireplace.
   - Have chimneys and wood stoves inspected annually and cleaned if necessary.
   - Use portable heaters only in well-ventilated rooms.

9. Keep matches and lighters up high, away from children, and if possible, in a locked cabinet.

10. Don't smoke in bed, or when drowsy or medicated. Provide smokers with deep, sturdy ashtrays. Douse cigarette and cigar butts with water before disposal.

11. Safety experts recommend that you sleep with your door closed.

12. Know the locations of the gas valve and electric fuse or circuit breaker box and how to turn them off in an emergency.

13. Put A-B-C type fire extinguishers in the home and teach family members how to use them

    - Type A — wood or papers fires only
    - Type B — flammable liquid or grease fires
    - Type C — electrical fires
    - Type A-B-C — rated for all fires and recommended for the home.

14. Consider installing an automatic fire sprinkler system in your home.

15. Ask your local fire department to inspect your residence for fire safety and prevention.

16. Teach children how to report a fire and when to use 911.

WHAT TO DO DURING A FIRE

1. Use water or a fire extinguisher to put out small fires.

   • Don't try to put out a fire that is getting out of control. If you're not sure if you can control it, get everyone out of the residence and call the fire department from a neighbor's residence.

2. Never use water on an electrical fire. Use only a fire extinguisher approved for electrical fires.

3. Smother oil and grease fires in the kitchen with baking soda or salt, or put a lid over the flame if it is burning in a pan. Don't try to take the pan outside.

4. If your clothes catch on fire, stop, drop and roll until the fire is extinguished. Running only makes the fire burn faster.

5. If you are escaping through a closed door, use the back of your hand to feel the top of the door, the doorknob, and the crack between the door and door frame before you open it. Never use the palm of your hand or fingers to test for heat. Burning those parts of your body could damage your ability to escape a fire (like using ladders and crawling).

   • If the door is cool, open slowly and make sure fire and/or smoke is not blocking your escape route. If your escape route is blocked, shut the door immediately and use an alternate escape route, such as a window. If clear, leave immediately through the door. Be prepared to crawl. Smoke and heat rise. The air is clearer and cooler near the floor.

   • If the door is warm or hot, don't open. Escape through a window. If you cannot escape, hang a white or light-colored sheet outside the window, showing fire fighters where you are.

6. If you must exit through smoke, crawl low under the smoke to your exit — heavy smoke and poisonous gases collect first along the ceiling.

7. Close doors behind you as you escape to delay the spread of the fire. If your clothes are on fire, stop, drop and roll until the fire is extinguished.

8. Once you are safely out, stay out. Call 911.

WHAT TO DO AFTER A FIRE

1. Give first aid where needed. After calling 911 or your local emergency number, cool and cover burns to reduce chance of further injury or infection.

2. Don't enter a fire-damaged building unless authorities say it is okay.

3. If you must enter a fire-damaged building, watch out for heat and smoke. If you detect either, leave immediately.

4. Have an electrician check your household wiring before the current is turned on.

5. Don't try to reconnect any utilities yourself. Leave this to the fire department and other authorities.

6. Beware of structural damage. Roofs and floors may be weakened and need repair.

7. Contact your local disaster relief service, such as the American Red Cross or Salvation Army, if you need housing, food or a place to stay.

8. Call your insurance agent.

   - Make a list of damage and losses. Pictures are helpful.
   - Keep records of clean-up and repair costs. Receipts are important for both insurance and income tax claims.
   - Don't throw away any damaged goods until an official inventory has been taken. Your insurance company takes all damages into consideration.

9. If you rent your property, contact the landlord.

10. Secure personal belongings or move them to another location.

11. Discard food, beverages and medicines that have been exposed to heat, smoke or soot. Refrigerators and freezers left closed hold their temperature for a short time. Don't try to refreeze food that has thawed.

12. If you have a safe or strong box, don't try to open it. It can hold intense heat for several hours. If the door is opened before the box has cooled, the contents could burst into flames.

13. If a building inspector says the building is unsafe and you must leave your home:

    - Ask local police to watch the property during your absence.
    - Pack identification, medicines, glasses, jewelry, credit cards, checkbooks, insurance policies and financial records if you can reach them safely.
    - Notify friends, relatives, police and fire departments, your insurance agent, the mortgage company, utility companies, delivery services, employers, schools and the post office of your whereabouts.

FLOODS

Even if you've never experienced a major flood, you ought to know what to do if floodwaters threaten your community.

WHAT TO DO BEFORE A FLOOD

1. Know the terms used to describe flooding:
   - Flood Watch — Flooding is possible in your area.
   - Flash Flood Watch — Flash flooding is possible.
   - Flood Warning — Flooding is occurring or will occur soon. If advised to evacuate, do so immediately.
   - Flash Flood Warning — A flash flood is occurring. Seek higher ground on foot immediately.

2. Find out what the local official flood warning signals are and what to do when you hear them.
   - Check with your local emergency manager or Red Cross chapter for evacuation procedures in your area.
   - Find out how much warning time you will have to leave your home before the flood reaches you.

3. Find out if any dams in your area are a hazard to you.

4. Buy a portable radio and extra batteries.

5. Be prepared to evacuate. Learn the safest route from your home or place of business to high, safe ground if you should have to evacuate in a hurry.

6. Talk to your family about flooding and prepare a flood response plan.
   - Plan a place to meet your household in case you are separated from one another in a disaster and cannot return home.
   - Identify a friend, relative or motel where you can go when you are asked to evacuate.
   - Choose an out-of-town contact for everyone to call to say they are okay.
   - Test-drive your evacuation route to be certain it will be passable when flooding is likely.

7. Prepare to survive on your own for at least three days.
   - Assemble a disaster supply kit.
   - Keep a stock of food and extra drinking water.

8. Know how to shut off electricity, gas and water at main switches and valves.

9. Consider purchasing flood insurance. Flood losses are not covered under homeowners insurance policies.

10. Take these steps now for protecting your property:
    - Make a record of your personal property. Take photographs or videotapes

of your belongings. Store these documents in a safe place.

- Keep important papers in a safe place away from your home.
- Elevate furnace, water heater, and electric panel to higher floors or the attic if they are exposed to possible flooding.
- Install "check valves" in sewer traps.
- Build levees, berms, and floodwalls to stop flood-water from entering the building.
- Seal walls in basements with water-proofing compounds.
- Install flood shields and other flood-proofing measures.
- If flooding in your area is from sewer backup or basement seepage, a water alarm can give you

If there is any possibility of a flash flood, move immediately to higher ground. Don't wait for instructions to move.

precious lead time before your belongings are damaged by floodwaters. A water alarm beeps when water touches it. Water alarms are available at hardware stores.

- If your flood protection level is over your top floor, store supplies at a friend's house away from the flood-prone area or take them with you in your car.
- Take pets to a kennel or friend's home on high ground. Health codes don't allow animals in public shelters.
- If you have enough warning time, move the contents of your home above the flood protection level or to another safe place.
- In hurricane-prone areas, protect against wind damage. Install hurricane shutters or plywood covers over your windows and doors, take down TV antennas, and securely tie down boats, garbage cans, and everything else left outdoors.
- Tape plastic around the cap to your well.
- Turn off the electricity, gas, oil and water.
- Lock your house.
- Follow your designated evacuation route to a place of shelter.
- If you're away from home stay alert to the possibility of flash flooding. If it is raining a lot, or if

Downed power lines

you are in a mountainous area, it's a good idea to keep listening to local radio or TV stations (not distant stations).

- If you hear about a flash flood watch for your area, it's a good idea to stay on high ground. If you hear a flash flood warning, climb to higher ground immediately. Leave your car, camping gear, or other belongings where they are. You may have only minutes to escape. Flash floods can happen without warning. If you hear a rumbling sound, if animals are running away from where you are, or if you feel the ground shaking, climb to higher ground immediately.

IF A FLOOD COMES

The safety of your family takes top priority. Since floodwaters can rise very rapidly, you should be prepared to evacuate before the water level reaches your property.

1. Keep your batter-powered portable radio tuned to a local station, and follow all emergency instructions.

2. If you're caught in the house by suddenly rising waters, move to the second floor and, if necessary, to the roof.

   - Take warm clothing, a flashlight, and a cellphone and portable radio with you. Then wait for help.
   - Don't try to swim to safety. Rescue teams will be looking for you.

3. Try to avoid flooded areas, and don't attempt to walk through floodwaters that are more than knee deep.

4. If, and only if, time permits, take these precautionary steps:

   - Turn off all utilities at the main power switch and close the main gas valve if it looks like you'll have to leave. Don't touch any electrical equipment unless it is in a dry area and you are standing on a piece of dry wood while wearing rubber gloves and rubber-soled boots or shoes.
   - Move valuables to upper floors or higher elevations.
   - If you have no second floor, don't worry. Water inside a building often gets no higher than two or three feet. Use high shelves for valuables including furnace motor.
   - Fill bathtubs, sinks and jugs with clean water in case regular supplies are contaminated. Sanitize these containers by first rinsing them with bleach.
   - Board up windows or protect them with storm shutters or tape to prevent flying glass.
   - Bring lawn furniture and tools inside the house or tie them down securely.

5. If it is safe to evacuate by car:

   - Stock the car with nonperishable foods (like canned goods), a plastic container of water, blankets, first-aid kit, flashlights, dry clothing and any special medication needed by your family.

- Keep the gas tank at least half full.
- Don't drive where the water is over the roads. Parts of the road may already be washed out.
- If your car stalls in a flooded area, abandon it as soon as possible. Floodwaters can rise rapidly and sweep a car (and its occupants) away.

WHAT TO DO AFTER A FLOOD

1. Avoid floodwaters. The water may be contaminated by oil, gasoline or raw sewage. The water may also be electrically charged from underground or downed power lines.

2. Avoid moving water. Moving water only six inches deep can sweep you off your feet.

3. Look out for spots where floodwaters have receded. Roads may have weakened and could collapse under the weight of a car.

4. Stay away from downed power lines and report them to the power company.

5. Stay away from designated disaster areas unless authorities ask for volunteers.

6. Return home only when authorities indicate it is safe.

- Stay out of the building if it is surrounded by floodwaters.
- Use extreme caution when entering building. There may be damage you can't see.
- Don't use open flame as a source of light since gas may still be trapped inside. Use a flashlight.
- Watch for electrical shorts or live wires before making certain that the main power switch is turned off. Don't turn on any lights or appliances until an electrician has checked the system for short circuits.

7. Remember your family's health and safety needs:

- Wash hands frequently with soap and clean water if you are exposed to floodwaters.
- Throw away food that has come in contact with floodwaters.
- Listen for news reports to learn whether the community's water supply is safe to drink.
- Get necessary medical care at the nearest hospital ER.

8. Fix damaged septic tanks, cesspools, pits, and leaching systems as soon as possible.

EXTREME WEATHER

HURRICANES

If you live near the coast, you will be asked to evacuate when a hurricane threatens your community. It is important to evacuate when you are asked to. You will need time to get ready. You will need time to board up your windows and to clear your yard so that your belongings will not blow or float away. You may also want to take time to move your belongings above the flood protection level.

WHAT TO DO BEFORE A HURRICANE

1. Know the difference between "Watches" and "Warnings."

   - Hurricane/Tropical Storm Watch — Hurricane/tropical storm conditions are possible in the specified area, usually within 36 hours.
   - Hurricane/Tropical Storm Warning — Hurricane/tropical storm conditions are expected in the specified area, usually within 24 hours.
   - Short Term Watches and Warnings — These warnings provide detailed information on specific hurricane threats, such as flash floods and tornadoes.

2. Listen for local radio or television weather forecasts. Buy a portable radio and extra batteries as well.

3. Ask your local emergency management office about community evacuation plans for your neighborhood.

Create a household disaster plan. Plan to meet your family in case you are separated. Choose an out-of-town contact for everyone to call to say they are safe.

   - Learn evacuation routes. Figure out where you would go and how you would get there. You may want to have alternate routes in mind as well.

4. Create a household disaster plan. Plan to meet at a place away from your home in case you are separated. Choose an out-of-town contact for everyone to call to say they are safe.

5. Find out the needs of your family members who may live elsewhere but who may need your help in a hurricane.

6. Prepare to survive on your own for at least three days.

   - Assemble a disaster supply kit. (See page 70.)
   - Keep a stock of food and extra drinking water.

7. Make plans to secure your property. Permanent storm shutters offer the best protection for windows.

8. Learn how to shut off utilities and where water mains are located.

9. Have your home inspected for compliance with local building codes.

10. Be sure trees and shrubs around your home are well-trimmed.

11. If you have a boat, secure it at the first sign of an emergency.

WHAT TO DO DURING A HURRICANE THREAT

1. Listen to radio or television newscasts. If a hurricane "Watch" is issued, you have 24 to 36 hours before the hurricane hits land.

2. Get together with family members. Make sure everyone knows where to meet and who to call in case you are separated.

3. Secure your home. Close storm shutters. Secure outdoor objects or bring them indoors. Moor your boat if time permits.

4. Gather several days' supply of water and food for each household member. Water systems may become contaminated or damaged. Sterilize (with diluted bleach solution of one part bleach to ten parts water) and fill the bathtub to ensure a supply of safe water in case you are unable or told not to evacuate.

5. If you are evacuating, take your disaster supply kit with you to the shelter.

6. Prepare to evacuate.
   - Fuel your car — service stations may be closed after the storm.
   - If you don't have a car, arrange for transportation with a friend or relative.
   - Review evacuation routes.
   - If instructed, turn off utilities at the main valves.

7. Evacuate to an inland location:
   - If local authorities announce an evacuation and you live in an evacuation zone.
   - If you live in a mobile home or temporary structure.
   - If you live in a high-rise. Hurricane winds are stronger at higher elevations.
   - If you live on the coast, on a floodplain near a river or inland waterway.
   - If you feel you are in danger.
8. When authorities order an evacuation:
   - Leave immediately.
   - Follow evacuation routes announced by local officials.
   - Stay away from coastal areas, river-banks and streams.
   - Tell others where you are going.
9. If you can't leave, stay indoors during the hurricane and away from windows and glass doors.

- Keep curtains and blinds closed.
- Turn off utilities if told to do so by authorities.
- If not instructed to turn it off, turn the refrigerator to its coldest setting and keep closed.

10. In strong winds, follow these rules:

- Hide in a small interior room, closet or hallway.
- Close all interior doors.
- Secure and brace external doors.
- In a two-story residence, go to an interior first-floor room, such as a bathroom or closet.
- In a multiple-story building, go to the first or second floors and stay in interior rooms away from windows.
- Lie on the floor under a table or another sturdy object.

11. Don't use the phone except for serious emergencies.

WHAT TO DO AFTER A HURRICANE

1. Stay where you are, if you are in a safe location, until local authorities say it is safe to leave.

- If you evacuated the community, don't return to the area until authorities say it is safe to return.
- Streets will be filled with debris.
- Roads may have weakened and could collapse.
- Don't drive on flooded or barricaded roads or bridges.

2. Keep tuned to local radio or television stations for information about caring for your household, where to find medical help, how to apply for financial assistance, etc.

3. Find out if any dams in your area are a hazard to you.

4. Don't drink or prepare food with tap water until notified by officials that it is safe to do so.

5. Talk with your children about what has happened and how they can help during the recovery. Being involved will help them deal with the situation.

6. Stay away from disaster areas unless local authorities request volunteers. If you are needed, bring your own drinking water, food and sleeping gear.

7. Stay away from riverbanks and streams until potential flooding has passed.

- Don't allow children to play in flooded areas. There is a high risk of injury or drowning in areas that may appear to be safe.

8. Stay away from moving water.

- Moving water only six inches deep can sweep you off your feet.

- Standing water may be electrically charged from underground or downed power lines.

9. Stay away from downed power lines and report them to the power company. Report broken gas, sewer or water mains to local officials.

10. Don't use candles or other open flames indoors. Use a flashlight to inspect damage.

THUNDERSTORMS

WHAT TO DO BEFORE THUNDERSTORMS APPROACH

1. Know the terms used by weather forecasters:

- Severe Thunderstorm Watch — Tells you when and where severe thunderstorms are likely to occur. Watch the sky and stay tuned to radio or television to know when warnings are issued.
- Severe Thunderstorm Warning — Issued when severe weather has been reported by spotters or indicated by radar. Warnings mean imminent danger to life and property to those in the path of the storm.

2. Remove dead or rotting trees and branches that could fall and cause injury or damage during a severe thunderstorm.

Get away from anything metal.

3. When a thunderstorm approaches, secure outdoor objects that could blow away or cause damage. Shutter windows, if possible, and secure outside doors. If shutters are not available, close window blinds, shades or curtains.

LIGHTNING

1. If you are inside a home:

- Avoid showering or bathing. Plumbing and bathroom fixtures can conduct electricity.
- Avoid using a corded telephone, except for emergencies. Cordless and cellular telephones are safer to use.
- Unplug appliances and other electrical items such as computers and turn off air conditioners. Power surges from lightning can cause serious damage.
- Use your portable radio for updates from local officials.

2. If outside, with no time to reach a safe location, follow these recommendations:

- In a forest, seek shelter in a low area under a thick growth of small trees.
- In open areas, go to a low place such as a ravine or valley. Be alert for flash floods.
- Don't stand under a natural lightning rod, such as a tall, isolated tree in an open area.

- Don't stand on a hilltop, in an open field, on the beach or in a boat on the water.
- Avoid isolated sheds or other small structures in open areas.
- Get away from open water. If you are boating or swimming, get to land and find shelter immediately.
- Get away from anything metal — tractors, farm equipment, beach umbrellas, motorcycles, golf carts, golf clubs and bicycles.
- Stay away from wire fences, clotheslines, metal pipes, rails and other metallic paths that could carry lightning to you from some distance away.
- If you feel your hair stand on end (which indicates that lightning is about to strike), squat low to the ground on the balls of your feet. Place your hands over your ears and your head between your knees. Make yourself the smallest target possible and minimize your contact with the ground. Don't lie flat on the ground.

Safety Tips:

- Postpone outdoor activities if thunderstorms are likely.
- Remember the 30/30 lightning safety rule — Go indoors if, after seeing lightning, you cannot count to 30 before hearing thunder. Stay indoors for 30 minutes after hearing the last clap of thunder.
- Rubber-soled shoes and rubber tires provide NO protection from lightning. However, the steel frame of a hard-topped vehicle provides increased protection if you are not touching metal. Although you may be injured if lightning strikes your car, you are much safer inside a vehicle than outside.

Lightning

TORNADOES

WHAT TO DO BEFORE TORNADOES THREATEN

1. Know the terms used to describe tornado threats:

   • Tornado Watch — Tornadoes are possible. Remain alert for approaching storms. Listen to your portable radio or battery-operated NOAA Weather Radio or local radio/television outlets for updated reports.
   • Tornado Warning — A tornado has been sighted or indicated by weather radar. Take shelter immediately.

2. Find out what your local warning signals are.

3. Buy a portable radio and extra batteries.

4. Know the name of the county or parish in which you live. Counties and parishes are used in Watches and Warnings to identify the location of tornadoes.

5. Determine places to seek shelter, such as a basement or storm cellar. If an underground shelter is not available, identify an interior room or hallway on the lowest floor.

6. Practice going to your shelter with your family.

7. Learn where the designated shelters are in places where you and your household spend time, such as public buildings, nursing homes and shopping centers.

8. Ask your local emergency manager or American Red Cross chapter if there are any public safe rooms or shelters nearby.

9. Assemble a disaster supplies kit. (See page 70.) Keep a stock of food and extra drinking water.

10. Make a record of your personal property. Take photographs or videotapes of your belongings. Store these documents in a safe place.

WHAT TO DO DURING A TORNADO WATCH

1. Listen to radio or television newscasts for the latest information.

2. Be alert for approaching storms. If you see any revolving funnel shaped clouds, report them immediately by telephone to your local police department or sheriff's office.

3. Watch for tornado danger signs:

   • Dark, often greenish sky
   • Large hailstones
   • A large, dark, low-lying cloud (particularly if rotating)
   • Loud roar, like that of a freight train

Caution:

- Some tornadoes are clearly visible, while rain or nearby low-hanging clouds obscure others.
- Occasionally, tornadoes develop so rapidly that little warning is possible.
- Before a tornado hits, the wind may die down and the air may become very still.
- A cloud of debris can mark the location of a tornado even if a funnel is not visible.
- Tornadoes generally occur near the trailing edge of a thunderstorm. It is not uncommon to see clear, sunlit skies behind a tornado.

4. Avoid places with wide-span roofs such as auditoriums, cafeterias, large hallways, supermarkets or shopping malls.

5. Be prepared to take shelter immediately. Gather household members and pets. Assemble supplies to take to the shelter such as flashlight, battery-powered radio, water and first-aid kit.

WHAT TO DO DURING A TORNADO WARNING

When a tornado has been sighted, go to your shelter immediately.

1. In a home or small building, move to a predesignated shelter, such as a basement or storm cellar.

2. If there is no basement, go to an inside room on the lower level (closets, interior hallways). Put as many walls as possible between you and the outside. Get under a sturdy table and use your arms to protect head and neck. Stay there until the danger has passed.

3. Don't spend precious time opening windows. Use the time to seek shelter.

4. Stay away from windows, doors and outside walls. Go to the center of the room. Stay away from corners because they attract debris.

5. In a school, nursing home, hospital, factory or shopping center, go to the shelter areas that have been set up.

- Interior hallways on the lowest floor are usually safest.
- Stay away from windows and open spaces.

6. In a high-rise building, go to a small, inside room or hallway on the lowest floor possible.

7. Get out of vehicles, trailers and mobile homes immediately and go to the lowest floor of a sturdy nearby building or a storm shelter.

- Mobile homes, even if tied down, offer little protection from tornadoes.

8. If caught outside with no shelter, lie flat in a nearby ditch or depression and cover your head with your hands. Look out for flooding.

9. Don't get under an overpass or bridge. You are safer in a low, flat location.

10. Never try to outrun a tornado in urban or congested areas in a car or truck. Instead, leave the vehicle immediately for safe shelter. Tornadoes are erratic and move swiftly.

11. Watch out for flying debris.

WHAT TO DO AFTER A TORNADO

1. Look out for broken glass and downed power lines.

2 Check for injuries. Don't attempt to move seriously injured persons unless they are in immediate danger.

- If you must move an unconscious person, first stabilize the neck and back, then call for help immediately.
- If the victim is not breathing, carefully position the victim for artificial respiration, clear the airway and begin assist breathing. (See page 10.).
- Maintain the victim's body temperature with blankets. Be sure the victim does not become overheated.
- Never try to feed liquids to an unconscious person.

3. Use caution when entering a damaged building. Be sure that walls, ceiling and roof are in place and that the structure rests firmly on the foundation. Wear sturdy work boots and gloves.

WINTER STORMS AND EXTREME COLD

WHAT TO DO BEFORE A WINTER STORM THREATENS

1. Know the terms used by weather forecasters:

- Freezing rain — Rain that freezes when it hits the ground, creating a coating of ice on roads, walkways, trees and power lines.
- Sleet — Rain that turns to ice pellets before reaching the ground. Sleet also causes roads to freeze and become slippery.
- Winter Storm Watch — A winter storm is possible in your area.
- Winter Storm Warning — A winter storm is occurring, or will soon occur in your area.
- Blizzard Warning — Sustained winds or frequent gusts to 35 miles-per-hour or greater and considerable falling or blowing snow (reducing visibility to less than a quarter mile) are expected to prevail for a period of three hours or longer.
- Frost/Freeze Warning — Below freezing temperatures are expected.

2. Prepare to survive on your own for at least three days. Assemble a disaster supply kit. Be sure to include items such as rock salt to melt ice on walkways, sand to improve traction, snow shovels and other snow removal equipment. Keep a stock of food and extra drinking water.

3. Prepare to be isolated in your home:

- Have enough heating fuel. Regular fuel sources may be cut off.
- Have emergency heating equipment and fuel (a gas fireplace or a wood-burning stove or fireplace) so you can keep at least one room of your residence livable. (Be sure the room is well ventilated.)
- If a thermostat controls your furnace and your electricity is cut off by a storm, you will need emergency heat.
- Store a good supply of dry, seasoned wood for your fireplace or wood-burning stove.
- Keep fire extinguishers on hand, and make sure your household knows how to use them.
- Never burn charcoal indoors.

4 Winterize your home to get the most from your fuel supply.

Winterize your home to get the most from your fuel supply.

- Insulate walls and attics.
- Caulk and weather-strip doors and windows
- Install storm windows or cover windows with plastic.

5. Maintain several days' supply of medicines, water and food that needs no cooking or refrigeration.

WHAT TO DO DURING A WINTER STORM

1. Listen to the radio or television for weather reports and emergency information.

2. Eat regularly and drink ample liquids, but avoid caffeine and alcohol.

3. Dress for the season:

- Wear several layers of loose fitting, lightweight, warm clothing rather than one layer of heavy clothing. The outer garments should be tightly woven and water repellent.
- Mittens are warmer than gloves.
- Wear a hat. Most body heat is lost through the top of the head.
- Cover your mouth with a scarf to protect your lungs.

4. Be careful when shoveling snow.

5. Watch for signs of frostbite.

6. Watch for signs of hypothermia.

7. When at home:

- Conserve fuel if necessary by keeping your home cooler than normal. Temporarily close off heat to some rooms.
- When using kerosene heaters, maintain ventilation to avoid build-up of toxic fumes.
- Refuel kerosene heaters outside and keep them at least three feet from flammable objects.

EARTHQUAKES

WHAT TO DO BEFORE AN EARTHQUAKE

1. Look for items in your home that could become hazards in an earthquake:

   - Repair defective electrical wiring, leaky gas lines and inflexible utility connections.
   - Bolt down water heaters and gas appliances (have an automatic gas shut-off device installed that is triggered by an earthquake).
   - Place large or heavy objects on lower shelves. Fasten shelves to walls. Brace high and top-heavy objects.
   - Store bottled foods, glass, china and other breakables on low shelves or in cabinets that can fasten shut.

   Hold earthquake drills with your family.

   - Anchor overhead lighting fixtures.
   - Check and repair deep plaster cracks in ceilings and foundations. Get expert advice, especially if there are signs of structural defects.
   - Be sure the house is firmly anchored to its foundation.
   - Install flexible pipe fittings to avoid gas or water leaks. Flexible fittings are less likely to break.

2. Know where and how to shut off electricity, gas and water at main switches and valves. Check with your local utilities for instructions.

3. Hold earthquake drills with your family:

   - Locate safe spots in each room under a sturdy table or against an inside wall. Reinforce this information by physically placing yourself and members of your household in these locations.
   - Identify danger zones in each room — near windows where glass can shatter, bookcases or furniture that can fall over, or under ceiling fixtures that could fall down.

4. Develop a plan for reuniting your family after an earthquake. Establish an out-of-town telephone contact for household members to call to let others know that they are okay.

5. Prepare to survive on your own for at least three days. Assemble a disaster supplies kit. (See page 70.) Keep a stock of food and extra drinking water.

WHAT TO DO DURING AN EARTHQUAKE

Stay inside until the shaking stops and it is safe to go outside. Most earthquake injuries occur when people are hit by falling objects when entering or exiting buildings.

1. Drop, Cover and Hold On! Minimize your movements during an earthquake to a few steps to a nearby safe place. Stay indoors until the shaking

has stopped and you are sure going out is safe.

2. If you are indoors, take cover under a sturdy desk, table or bench, or against an inside wall, and hold on. Stay away from glass, windows, outside doors or walls and anything that could fall, such as lighting fixtures or furniture. If you are in bed, stay there, hold on and protect your head with a pillow.

3. If there isn't a table or desk near you, cover your face and head with your arms and crouch in an inside corner of the building. Doorways should only be used for shelter if you're near them and if you know that it is a strongly supported load-bearing doorway.

4. If you are outdoors, stay there. Move away from buildings, streetlights and utility wires. Remain calm.

5. If you are in an apartment house or another building with many floors, do the following:

   • Get under a desk and stay away from windows and outside walls.
   • Stay in the building.
   • Be aware that the electricity may go out and sprinkler systems may come on.
   • DON'T use the elevators.

6. If you are in a crowded indoor public location:

   • Stay where you are. Do not rush for the doorways.
   • Move away from tall shelves, cabinets and bookcases.
   • Take cover and grab something to shield your head and face from falling debris and glass.
   • Be aware that the electricity may go out or the sprinkler systems or fire alarms may turn on.
   • DON'T use elevators.

7. Stay indoors until the shaking has stopped and you are sure it's safe to leave.

8. In a moving vehicle, stop as quickly as safety permits, and stay in the vehicle. Don't stop near or under buildings, trees, overpasses or utility wires. Then proceed cautiously, watching for road and bridge damage.

9. If you become trapped in debris:

   • Don't light a match.
   • Don't move about or kick up dust.
   • Cover your mouth with a handkerchief or clothing.
   • Tap on a pipe or wall so rescuers can locate you.
   • Use a whistle if one is available.
   • Shout only as a last resort — shouting can cause you to inhale dangerous amounts of dust.

WHAT TO DO AFTER AN EARTHQUAKE

1. Be prepared for aftershocks. These can do more damage to weakened structures.

2. Check for injuries. Don't attempt to move seriously injured persons unless they are in immediate danger of death or further injury. If you must move an unconscious person, first stabilize the neck and back, then call for help immediately.

   - If the victim is not breathing, start assist breathing. (See page 10.)
   - Maintain body temperature with blankets.
   - Never try to feed liquids to an unconscious person.

3. If the electricity goes out, use flashlights or battery powered lanterns. Don't use candles, matches or open flames indoors after the earthquake because of possible gas leaks.

4. Wear sturdy shoes in areas covered with fallen debris and broken glass. If you must go out after an earthquake, watch for fallen objects, downed electrical wires, weakened walls, bridges, roads and sidewalks.

5. Check your home for structural damage .

6. Check chimneys for visual damage. Have a professional inspect the chimney for internal damage before lighting a fire.

7. Clean up spilled medicines, bleaches, gasoline and other flammable liquids. Evacuate the building if gasoline fumes are detected and the building is not well ventilated.

8. Visually inspect utility lines and appliances for damage.

   - If you smell gas or hear a hissing or blowing sound, open a window and leave.
   - Shut off the main gas valve. Report the leak to the gas company from the nearest working phone or cell phone available.
   - Stay out of the building.
   - Switch off electrical power at the main fuse box or circuit breaker if electrical damage is suspected or known.
   - Shut off the water supply at the main valve if water pipes are damaged.
   - Don't flush toilets until you know that sewage lines are intact.

9. Open cabinets cautiously. Beware of objects that can fall off shelves.

10. Use the phone only to report life-threatening emergencies.

11. Listen to news reports for the latest emergency information.

12. Stay off the streets. If you must go out, watch for fallen objects, downed electrical wires, weakened walls, bridges, roads and sidewalks.

13. Stay away from the damage zone unless your assistance has been specifically requested by police, fire or relief organizations.

14. If you live in a coastal area, stay away from the beach.

VOLCANOES

WHAT TO DO BEFORE AN ERUPTION

1. Make evacuation plans. If you live in a known volcanic hazard area, plan a route out and have a backup route in mind.

2. Develop a household disaster plan. In case household members are separated from one another during a volcanic eruption, have a plan for getting back together.

   • Ask an out-of-town relative or friend to serve as the "household contact," because after a disaster, it's often easier to call long distance.
   • Make sure everyone knows the name, address, and phone number of the contact person.

3. Assemble a disaster supply kit.

4. Get a pair of goggles and a throw-away breathing mask for each member of the household in case of ashfall.

5. Don't visit an active volcano site unless officials designate a safe viewing area.

WHAT TO DO DURING AN ERUPTION

1. Get away immediately from the volcano.

2. Avoid areas downwind from the volcano to avoid volcanic ash.

3. Look out for mudflows.

WHAT TO DO AFTER THE ERUPTION

1. Avoid ashfall areas if possible. If you are in an ashfall area, cover your mouth and nose with a mask. Keep skin covered, and wear goggles to protect the eyes.

2. Clear roofs of ashfall.

3. Avoid driving through ashfall.

4. If you have a respiratory ailment, avoid contact with any amount of ash. Stay indoors until local health officials advise it is safe to go outside.

5. Stay indoors until the ash has settled unless there is danger of the roof collapsing.

6. During an ashfall, close doors, windows and all ventilation.

7. Don't drive in heavy dust unless absolutely required.

8. Follow these precautions to keep safe from ashfall:

   • Wear long-sleeved shirts and long pants.
   • Use goggles and wear eyeglasses instead of contact lenses.
   • Use a dust mask or hold a damp cloth over your face to breathe easier.

TECHNOLOGICAL AND MAN-MADE HAZARDS

Hazardous Materials Incidents

Here is what to do in case a hazardous materials situation arises in your area. This could include accidents like a tanker truck filled with dangerous materials spilling over in your community, or a derailed box car leaking its explosive contents, or a nearby nuclear power plant possibly leaking radiation, or a gas main explosion nearby.

WHAT TO DO BEFORE A HAZARDOUS MATERIALS INCIDENT

1. Ask your fire or police department about warning procedures. These could include:

   - Outdoor warning sirens or horns.
   - Emergency Alert System (EAS)— Information given on radio and television.
   - "All-Call" telephoning — An automated system for sending recorded messages.
   - News media — Radio, television and cable.
   - Residential route alerting — Messages announced to neighborhoods from vehicles equipped with public address systems.

2. Find out what the local plans are for responding to a hazardous materials accident at a plant or other facility.

Find out what the local plans are for responding to hazardous materials accidents at plants or other facilities.

• If you witness a hazardous materials accident, call 911, your local emergency notification number or the fire department.

3. Ask your local authorities if hazardous chemicals are being stored or used in your area.

4. Find out how close you are to factories, freeways or railroads that may produce or transport toxic waste.

5. Be prepared to evacuate. An evacuation could last for a few hours or several days.

6. Be prepared to seek safety in your home or any other building you might be in at the time of a chemical release.

   - At home you should select a room to be used as a shelter. This place should be above ground, large enough to accommodate all household members and pets. It should have the fewest possible windows and doors leading to the outside.
   - You should also put together a shelter kit to be used to seal the shelter room during a chemical release. The kit should include plastic sheeting, duct tape, scissors, a towel and modeling clay or other material to stuff into cracks.

WHAT TO DO DURING A HAZARDOUS MATERIALS INCIDENT

1. If you see (or smell) a hazardous materials accident, call 911, your local emergency notification number, or the fire department as soon as it's safe for you to do so.

2. If you hear a warning signal, listen to local radio or television stations for further information. Follow instructions carefully.

3. Stay away from the incident site to lower the risk of contamination.

4. If you are caught outside during an incident, remember that gases and mists are generally heavier than air. Try to stay upstream, uphill and upwind — hazardous materials can quickly be transported by water and wind.

   • In general, try to go at least one-half mile (10 city blocks) from the danger area. For many incidents you will need to go much further.

5. If you are in a car, stop and seek shelter in a permanent building if possible. If you must remain in your car, keep car windows and vents closed and shut off the air conditioner and heater.

6. If asked to evacuate your home, do so immediately.

   • If authorities say there is enough time, close all windows, shut vents and turn off attic, heating and air conditioning fans to lower contamination.

   • An evacuation could last for a few hours or several days. Be prepared in advance.

7. If you are requested to stay indoors rather than evacuate:

   • Follow all instructions given by emergency authorities.
   • Get household members and pets inside as quickly as possible.
   • Close and lock all windows and doors leading to the outside. Close vents, fireplace dampers and as many interior doors as possible.
   • Turn off air conditioners and ventilation systems.
   • Go into the pre-selected shelter room. This is the room you've picked that's above ground and which has the fewest openings to the outside.
   • Take a battery-powered radio, water, sanitary supplies, a flashlight and a shelter kit containing plastic sheeting, duct tape, scissors, a towel and modeling clay or other materials to stuff into cracks.
   • Close doors and windows in the room.
   • Stuff a towel tightly under each door and tape around the sides and top of the door.
   • Cover each window and vent in the room with a single piece of plastic sheeting, taping all around the edges of the sheeting to provide a continuous seal.
   • If there are any cracks or holes in the room, such as those around pipes entering a bathroom, fill them with modeling clay or other similar material.

- Remain in the room, listening to emergency broadcasts on the radio, until authorities tell you it's safe to leave your shelter.
- If authorities warn of the possibility of an outdoor explosion, close all drapes, curtains and shades in the room.
- Stay away from windows to prevent injury from breaking glass.
- When authorities advise people in your area to leave their shelters, open all doors and windows and turn on air conditioning and ventilation systems. These measures will flush out any chemicals that infiltrated into the building.

8. If there is a hazardous materials incident and your children are at school, you will probably not be permitted to drive to the school to pick up your children. Even if you go to the school, the doors will probably be locked to keep your children safe. Follow the directions of your local emergency officials.

9. Avoid contact with spilled liquids, air-borne mists or condensed solid chemical deposits.

- Keep your body fully covered to provide some protection. Wear gloves, socks, shoes, long skirts, pants and long sleeved shirts.

10. Don't eat or drink food or water that may have been contaminated.

11. If indoors, sterilize the bathtub with a diluted bleach solution — one part bleach to ten parts water. Carefully drain out the solution. You can then fill the bathtub and large containers with water for drinking, cooking, and dishwashing. Be prepared to turn off the main water intake valve in case authorities advise you to do so.

WHAT TO DO AFTER AN INCIDENT

Nearby accidents

1. Don't return home until local authorities say it is safe.

2. Upon returning home, open windows, vents and turn on fans to provide ventilation.

3. If you have come in contact with or have been exposed to hazardous chemicals, you should:

- Follow decontamination instructions from local authorities.
- Seek medical treatment for unusual symptoms as soon as possible.
- If medical help is not immediately available and you think you might be

contaminated, remove all of your clothing and shower thoroughly (unless local authorities say the chemical is water reactive and advise you to do otherwise).

- Change into fresh, loose clothing and seek medical help as soon as possible.
- Place exposed clothing and shoes in tightly sealed containers. Don't allow them to contact other materials. Call local authorities to find out about proper disposal.
- Advise everyone who comes in contact with you that you may have been exposed to a toxic substance.

4. Find out from local authorities how to clean up your land and property.

5. Report any lingering vapors or other hazards to your local emergency services office.

HEAT WAVE

WHAT TO DO BEFORE AN EXTREME HEAT EMERGENCY

1. Know the terms associated with extreme heat:

- Heat wave — Prolonged period of excessive heat, often with excessive humidity.
- Heat index — A number that tells how hot it feels. Exposure to full sunshine can increase the heat index by 15 degrees.
- Heat cramps — Muscular pains and spasms due to heavy exertion.
- Heat exhaustion — Occurs when people exercise heavily or work in a hot, humid place where body fluids are lost through heavy sweating. Body temperature will keep rising and the victim may suffer heat stroke.
- Heat stroke — Heat stroke is life-threatening. The victim's temperature control system, which produces sweating to cool the body, stops working.
- Sun stroke — Another term for heat stroke.

2. Here is what to do when faced with extreme heat:

- Install window air conditioners snugly; insulate if necessary.
- Close any floor heat registers nearby and use a circulating or box fan to spread cool air.
- Check air-conditioning ducts for proper insulation.
- Install temporary reflectors, such as aluminum foil covered cardboard, to reflect heat back outside. Be sure to weather-strip doors and sills to keep cool air in.
- Cover windows that receive morning or afternoon sun with drapes, shades, awnings or louvers. Outdoor awnings or louvers can reduce the heat that enters a home by up to 80 percent. Keep storm windows up all year.

WHAT TO DO DURING EXTREME HEAT OR A HEAT WAVE EMERGENCY

1. Stay indoors as much as possible. If air conditioning is not available, stay on the lowest floor out of the sunshine.

   • Remember that electric fans don't cool. They just blow hot air around.

2. Eat well-balanced, light and regular meals. Avoid using salt tablets unless a doctor tells you to.

3. Drink plenty of water regularly even if you don't feel thirsty, unless your doctor says otherwise.

4. Never leave children or pets alone in closed vehicles.

5. Dress in loose-fitting clothes that cover as much skin as possible.

   • Lightweight, light-colored clothing reflects heat and sunlight and helps maintain normal body temperature.

6. Protect face and head by wearing a wide-brimmed hat.

7. Avoid too much sunshine.

   • Sunburn slows the skin's ability to cool itself. Use a sunscreen lotion with a high SPF (sun protection factor) rating (i.e., 15 or greater).

8. Avoid strenuous work during the warmest part of the day.

   • Use a buddy system when working in extreme heat and take frequent breaks.

9. Spend at least two hours per day in an air-conditioned place. If your home is not air conditioned, consider spending the warmest part of the day in public buildings such as libraries, schools, movie theaters, or shopping malls.

10. Check on family, friends, and neighbors who don't have air-conditioning and who spend much of their time alone.

11. Conserve electricity during periods of extreme heat. People tend to use a lot more power for air-conditioning, which could lead to a power shortage or outage.

12. For first aid for heat-induced illnesses, see page 47.

Heat Emergency

99

EMERGENCY WATER SHORTAGE

An emergency water shortage can be caused by prolonged drought or poor water supply management. A drought is a period of abnormally dry weather. Conserving water is very important during emergency water shortages.

Water conservation

1. Practice indoor water conservation:

   • Never pour water down the drain when there may be another use for it. Use it to water your indoor plants or garden.
   • Repair dripping faucets by replacing washers. One drop per second wastes 2,700 gallons of water per year!
   • Check all plumbing for leaks. Have leaks repaired by a plumber.

   Bathroom

   • Install a toilet displacement device to cut down on the amount of water needed to flush. Place a one-gallon plastic jug of water into the tank to displace toilet flow. (Don't use a brick which may dissolve. Loose pieces may cause damage to the internal parts.) Be sure installation does not interfere with the operating parts.
   • Consider purchasing a low-volume toilet that uses less than half the water of older models. NOTE: In many areas, low-volume units are required by law.
   • Replace your showerhead with an ultra-low-flow version.
   • Take short showers — only turn on water to get wet and lathered and then again to rinse off.
   • Place a bucket in the shower to catch excess water for watering plants.
   • Don't let the water run while brushing your teeth, washing your face or shaving.
   • Don't flush the toilet unnecessarily.

   Kitchen

   • Operate automatic dishwashers only when they are fully loaded. Use the "light wash" feature if available to use less water.
   • Hand wash dishes by filling two containers — one with soapy water and the other with rinse water containing a small amount of chlorine bleach.
   • Don't rinse dishes before putting them in the dishwasher.
   • Store drinking water in the refrigerator. Don't let the tap run while you are waiting for water to cool.
   • Don't waste water waiting for it to get hot. Capture it for other uses such as plant watering or heat it on the stove or in a microwave.
   • Don't use running water to thaw meat or other frozen foods. Defrost food overnight in the refrigerator, or use the defrost setting on your microwave.

- Clean vegetables in a pan filled with water rather than running water from the tap.
- Kitchen sink disposals require a lot of water to operate properly. Start a compost pile or dispose of food in the garbage.
- If you are considering installing a new heat pump or air-conditioning system, the new air-to-air models are just as efficient as the water-to-air type and don't waste water.
- Install a water-softening system only when the minerals in the water would damage your pipes. Turn the softener off while on vacation.
- When purchasing a new appliance, choose one that is more energy and water efficient.

2. Practice outdoor water conservation.

Car washing

- Use a shut-off nozzle on your hose that can be adjusted down to a fine spray, so that water flows only as needed.
- Consider using a commercial car wash that recycles water. If you wash your own car, park on the grass so that you will be watering it at the same time.

Lawn Care

- Don't over-water your lawn. A heavy rain eliminates the need for watering for up to two weeks. Most of the year, lawns only need one inch of water per week.
- Water in several short sessions rather than one long one in order for your lawn to better absorb moisture.
- Position sprinklers so water lands on the lawn and shrubs and not on paved areas.
- Avoid sprinklers that spray a fine mist. Mist can evaporate before it reaches the lawn.
- Check sprinkler systems and timing devices regularly to be sure they operate properly.
- Raise the lawn mower blade to at least three inches, or to its highest level. A higher cut encourages grass roots to grow deeper, shades the root system and holds soil moisture.
- Plant drought-resistant lawn seed.
- Avoid over-fertilizing your lawn. Applying fertilizer increases the need for water.
- Use a broom or blower instead of a hose to clean leaves and other debris from your driveway or sidewalk.
- Don't leave sprinklers or hoses unattended. A garden hose can pour out 600 gallons or more in only a few hours.

Pool

- Consider installing a new water-saving pool filter. A single back flushing with a traditional filter uses 180 to 250 gallons of water.
- Cover pools and spas to reduce evaporation of water.

WILDLAND FIRES

If you live on a remote hillside, or in a valley, prairie or forest where flammable vegetation is abundant, your home could be vulnerable to wildland fire. These fires are usually triggered by lightning or accidents.

1. Fire facts about rural living:

   • Once a fire starts outdoors in a rural area, it is often hard to control. Wildland firefighters are trained to protect natural resources, not homes and buildings.
   • Many homes are located far from fire stations.
   • Limited water supply in rural areas can make fire suppression difficult.
   • Homes may be secluded and surrounded by woody growth that fuels fires.

2. Ask fire authorities to inspect your residence and property for hazards.

3. Be prepared and have a fire safety and evacuation plan:

   • Practice fire escape and evacuation plans.
   • Mark the entrance to your property with address signs that are clearly visible from the road.
   • Keep the numbers of local emergency services posted near telephones.
   • Provide emergency vehicle access through roads and driveways at least 12 feet wide with adequate turn-around space.

4. Tips for making your property fire resistant:

   • Keep lawns trimmed, leaves raked, and the roof and rain-gutters free from debris such as dead limbs and leaves.
   • Stack firewood at least 30 feet away from your home.
   • Store flammable materials, liquids and solvents in metal containers outside your home at least 30 feet away from structures and wooden fences.
   • Create defensible space by thinning trees and brush within 30 feet around your home. Beyond 30 feet, remove dead wood and debris.
   • Landscape your property with fire resistant plants and vegetation to prevent fire from spreading quickly. For example, hardwood trees are more fire-resistant than pine, evergreen, eucalyptus or fir trees.
   • Make sure water sources are accessible to the fire department.

5. Protect your home:

   • Use fire resistant, protective roofing and materials like stone, brick and metal to protect your home. Avoid using wood materials.
   • Cover all exterior vents, attics and eaves with metal mesh screens.
   • Install multi-pane windows, tempered safety glass or fireproof shutters.
   • Use fire-resistant draperies for added window protection.
   • Have chimneys, wood stoves and all home heating systems inspected and

cleaned annually by a certified specialist.

- Insulate chimneys and place spark arresters on top. Chimneys should be at least three feet above the roof.
- Remove branches hanging above and around the chimney.

6. Follow local burning laws:

   - Before burning debris in a wooded area, obtain a burning permit.
   - Use an approved incinerator with a safety lid or covering with holes no larger than 3/4 inch.
   - Clear at least 10 feet around the incinerator before burning debris.
   - Have a fire extinguisher or garden hose on hand when burning debris.

7. If wildfire threatens your home and time permits, do the following:

Inside
- Shut off gas at the meter.
- Turn off pilot lights.
- Open fireplace damper. Close fireplace screens.
- Close windows, vents, doors, blinds or noncombustible window coverings, and heavy drapes. Remove flammable drapes and curtains.
- Move flammable furniture into the center of the home.
- Close all interior doors and windows to prevent drafts.
- Place valuables that will not be damaged by water in a pool or pond.
- Gather pets into one room. Make plans to care for your pets if you must evacuate.
- Back your car into the garage or park it in an open space facing the direction of escape. Shut doors and roll up windows. Leave the key in the ignition and the car doors unlocked. Close garage windows and doors, but leave them unlocked. Disconnect automatic garage door openers.

Outside
- Seal attic and ground vents with pre-cut plywood or commercial seals.
- Turn off propane tanks.
- Place combustible patio furniture inside.
- Connect garden hose to outside taps. Place lawn sprinklers on the roof and near above-ground fuel tanks. Wet the roof.
- Wet or remove shrubs within 15 feet of the home.
- Gather fire tools such as a rake, axe, handsaw or chainsaw, bucket and shovel.

8. If advised to evacuate, do so immediately. Choose a route away from the fire hazard. Watch for changes in the speed and direction of fire and smoke.

4 FOOD ALERTS

FOOD POISONING

Most food poisoning is caused by harmful bacteria. These can poison food that's been insufficiently cooked, improperly refrigerated, or left out too long. Food poisoning can be serious, especially for kids and older people. Food poisoning includes botulism, campylobacter poisoning, coccidian parasite infections, E. Coli infections, mushroom poisoning, salmonella poisoning, shigella poisoning, and staphylococcus poisoning. Most of these can be treated the same way. Botulism and mushroom poisoning have different treatments.

I. FOOD POISONING IN GENERAL

WHAT TO LOOK FOR

- Diarrhea
- Nausea
- Abdominal pain and cramps
- Vomiting

Prevent food poisoning

WHAT YOU SHOULD DO

1. Prevent dehydration — loss of body fluids.

   a. Give the victim drinks like Gatorade®, 7 UP®, apple juice, broth, bouillon or Pedialyte®. The person should take only small but frequent sips.

2. If victim shows signs of bloody diarrhea, call 911 or operator (0) or EMS.

3. Report any restaurant food poisoning to your county public health department.

WHAT YOU SHOULD **NOT** DO

- •☞ **DON'T** try to make the victim vomit.

II. BOTULISM

People can get botulism from eating improperly processed foods. When home-canning isn't done right, it can be a cause of botulism. Botulism is a very dangerous form of food poisoning.

WHAT TO LOOK FOR

- Blurred or double vision
- Large dark pupils in the center of the eye
- Droopy eyelids
- Headache
- Dry, sore mouth and throat
- Muscle weakness
- Difficulty swallowing and speaking
- Difficult breathing
- Paralysis

Be extra-careful when canning foods at home.

WHAT YOU SHOULD DO

Call 911 or operator (0) or EMS immediately.

WHAT YOU SHOULD NOT DO

☞ **DON'T** try to make person vomit.

What You Can Do to Avoid Botulism

- Be extra-careful when canning foods at home. Follow home canning directions exactly.
- When doing your shopping, stay away from any can that's bent, dented, broken, rusty, leaky or bulging.
- Throw out any food that explodes or sprays from a can when it is being opened
- When you come across a can that's lost its label or one you forgot about in the back of the refrigerator, remember the motto: "When in doubt, throw it out."
- Avoid canned food that is soft, deteriorating, fermenting or doesn't smell right.
- Never taste suspicious foods for any reason.

III. MUSHROOM POISONING

Certain mushrooms growing in the wild can be poisonous. It's a good idea not to go mushroom picking.

WHAT TO LOOK FOR

- Stomach pain
- Bloody diarrhea
- Bloody vomit
- Hard to breath
- Sweating
- Dizziness
- Muscle spasms
- Hallucinations

WHAT YOU SHOULD DO

1. Call 911 or operator (0) or EMS or the Poison Control Center immediately. Until help comes:

2. Follow the instructions of the emergency professionals on the phone.

3. Have victim lie down quietly.

WHAT YOU SHOULD NOT DO

☛ **DON'T** give mustard or table salt to make victim vomit.

Follow These Rules To Help Prevent Food Poisoning:

• Wash your hands before, during and after food preparation. Use soap and warm water and wash for at least 20 seconds.

• Use hot, soapy water to wash everything used to prepare food.

• Use a diluted bleach solution to clean cutting boards and countertops.

• Tip: Use the microwave to clean kitchen sponges and dishcloths. First rinse them in water and squeeze out the water. Then microwave at full power for 60 seconds. They're going to be hot, so be careful when taking out of the microwave.

• Use soap, water and paper towels to clean surfaces that have touched raw meat, fish or chicken. Don't use a sponge or dishcloth.

• Wash all fruits and vegetables before eating.

• Don't spill juice from raw meat on other foods.

• Cook all food thoroughly.

• Don't eat raw eggs.

• Wear gloves when preparing foods if you have cuts on your hands.

• Refrigerate all leftovers as soon as you can.

• Refrigerate frozen food as soon as possible.

• Throw out any food if you cannot remember when it was placed in the refrigerator.

• Check food to see that it hasn't gotten moldy, slimy or rotten.

• Keep refrigerator between 35-40° F and freezer at 0° F or lower.

• Cook red meat to 160° F. Large cuts can be cooked to 145° F.

• Cook ground meat and hamburgers all the way through until the center is at least 160-165° F.

• Cook fish to 130-140° F.

• Cook pork to 155° F with no pink showing.

• Cook chicken to 170-180° F, or until the juices run clear.

• Cook eggs until both the yolk and the white are firm.

• Heat leftovers to 165° F.

• Reheat sauces, soups and gravies to a boil.

• Don't eat raw cookie dough that contains eggs.

• Don't eat raw flounder, rockfish, salmon or sole.

5 EMERGENCIES ON THE ROAD

DRIVING AND ACCIDENTS

Here's how to handle emergencies when they happen.

If steam begins to come from under the hood, your cooling system is boiling. You should:

1. Pull to the side of the road and turn off the engine. Don't open the radiator cap.

If smoke comes from under the hood:

1. First check the traffic behind you.

2. Drive off the road clear of traffic and stop.

3. Turn off the engine and all electrical switches.

Remove rings and other jewelry when working on a car battery.

4. Get all passengers out of and away from the vehicle. Toxic fumes may fill the vehicle.

5. If the fire is small, use a chemical fire extinguisher, dirt, mud, sand, floor mat or even clothing to smother the fire.

   a. Don't use water on gasoline, oil or electrical fires.

6. If a large gasoline or oil fire develops, get help.

Jump-starting your car's dead battery from another car's battery could be dangerous. Either battery could explode and hurt you.

Car Battery Safety Tips

1. Never smoke or light a match around a car battery.

2. Remove rings and other jewelry when working on a car battery.

3. Using battery jump cables improperly can cause an explosion or ruin your alternator.

4. Wear goggles to keep acid from splashing into your eyes.

5. Work in a well-ventilated area.

6. If you get battery acid on your skin, eyes or car, wash it off immediately with water.

7. Check in with a doctor. (See chemical burns on eyes, page 35.)

If your car breaks down, slow down and pull off the pavement as far as possible. Warn motorists you're stuck by doing all of the following:

1. At night, if you have flares, put them at least 100 feet behind your car at the side of the road. Also put flares beside and 100 feet ahead of your car and at the side of the road for added safety.

2. During the day, tie a white cloth to the radio antenna or left door handle and raise the hood as a signal that your car has broken down.

3. Except for an emergency, stay with your car.

4. When traveling alone at night, stay in the car with the windows closed and the doors locked. Be cautious of anybody who offers help. If in doubt, remain locked inside the car and ask that police be notified.

5. If you pull over to the side of the road in fog, remember to turn on your hazard-warning flashers. A steady glow from parking lights may make a driver behind you think that you are moving along also and he may plow right into you.

Road Emergency Tool Kit

- Adjustable wrench
- 2-feet x 1-foot board (base for jack)
- Distress flag
- Duct tape
- Emergency flares
- Flashlight and spare batteries
- Gallon plastic jug
- Insulated screwdrivers: one Phillips head, one standard
- Insulated slip-joint, locking, and needle-nose pliers
- Jack
- Jumper cables
- Light that plugs into cigarette lighter
- Lug wrench; length of pipe to fit over end of wrench
- Penetrating oil
- Quart of engine oil
- Scrap electrical wire
- Spare clamp
- Spare fan belt
- Spare fuse kit and fuse puller
- Spare radiator hose

Except for an emergency, stay with your car.

Driving emergency

- Squeeze-type siphon to pump gas
- Tire sealant-inflator
- Utility knife
- Wheel chock
- Work gloves

TRAFFIC ACCIDENTS

The first thing to do in a traffic accident is to stop the car.

1. Have someone warn approaching traffic to prevent further damage.

2. Help the injured.

3. Call the police and ask for an ambulance if needed.

4. Don't move injured persons unless absolutely necessary.

5. Try to help the injured where they lie in order of their needs.

6. Loosen their clothing.

7. Keep them warm.

8. To stop bleeding, place a clean cloth over the wound. (See page 17.)

9. If a person has stopped breathing, give assist breathing. (See page 10.)

10. Have any walking injured person sit or lie down on his back.

   a. If the person is bleeding from the lower part of the face or jaw, turn him on his side.

   b. Don't give fluids.

 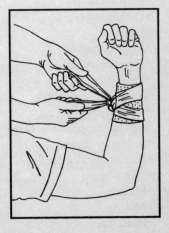

Bleeding

DRIVING IN BAD CONDITIONS

WINTER DRIVING

1. Don't travel alone.

2. Keep others informed of your schedule.

3. Stay on main roads. Avoid back-road shortcuts.

4. Winterize your car. This includes:

    •Battery check
    •Antifreeze
    •Wipers and windshield washer fluid
    •Ignition system
    •Thermostat
    •Lights
    •Flashing hazard lights
    •Exhaust system
    •Heater
    •Brakes
    •Defroster
    •Oil level
    •Snow tires, snow tires with studs or chains.

Keep the exhaust pipe cleared of snow. This is very important.

5. Keep your car's gas tank full.

6. Carry a "winter car kit" in the trunk of your car. The kit should include:

    •Shovel
    •Windshield scraper
    •Portable radio
    •Flashlight
    •Candles
    •Extra batteries
    •Bag of road salt
    •Blanket
    •Booster cables
    •Sleeping bag
    •Cellular telephone or two-way radio
    •Emergency flares
    •Fluorescent distress flag
    •Warm hat
    •Mittens
    •Matches
    •Road maps

- Trail mix
- Tire chains
- Tow chain or rope
- Water
- Sand

WHAT TO DO IF TRAPPED BY A BLIZZARD

- Pull off the highway. Turn on flashers and hang a distress flag from the radio aerial or window.
- If you're jammed in a drift and neither doors nor windows will open, push out the windshield or rear window with your feet.
- Stay in your car where rescuers are most likely to find you. Don't set out on foot unless you can see a safe place close by where you know you can take shelter.
- Avoid over exertion and exposure. Stay put. Think things out carefully.
- If you need something from the trunk, the lock will probably be frozen. Have your cigarette lighter ready to thaw it.
- Run the engine and heater sparingly in ten minute periods every hour to keep warm.
- When the engine is running, open your downwind window slightly for ventilation. This will protect you from carbon monoxide fumes. Also keep the exhaust pipe cleared of snow. This is very important.
- Shake off all wet snow before reentering the car. You have to keep as dry as possible inside the car. Carry some covering like rubber floor mats held over your shoulders as a form of umbrella.
- Clap your hands and move your arms and legs vigorously from time to time to maintain body heat and keep from getting stiff, but avoid overexertion. Don't stay in one position for too long. In extreme cold, use road maps, seat covers and floor mats for insulation.
- Huddle with passengers and use your coat for a blanket.
- Take turns sleeping. Don't let everybody in the car sleep at the same time. Take turns in keeping awake to keep an eye out for rescue crews.
- Drink fluids to avoid dehydration.
- Be careful not to waste battery power.
- At night, turn on the dome light so work crews or rescuers can see you.
- If stranded in a remote area, spread a large cloth over the snow to attract attention of rescue personnel who may be surveying the area by air.

OTHER BAD WEATHER DRIVING

Earthquake

- Park away from tall buildings, trees, bridges, overpasses.

- Don't leave the car.
- Dive for the floor and stay there.
- Stay below seat level.
- After quake ends, continue on your way.

Strong winds
- Grip the steering wheel firmly.
- Cut down speed.

Tornadoes
- Pull over.
- Get out and find a ditch to lie in.

If you have a passenger air bag, don't put your child in the front seat.

DRIVING AND CHILDREN

- Don't let your child play with the windows.
- Have your child get out of the car on the curb side.
- Never leave a young child alone in a car.
- Remove the cigarette lighter.
- Use child locks on rear doors.
- Watch for little fingers when you shut the doors.
- Make sure that children under the age of 12 ride in the backseat.
- Use car seats for infants and toddlers under 40 pounds.
- Use a special safety seat when you strap your child into the car.
- Babies up to 20 pounds should travel in a rear-facing car seat.
- Babies over 20 pounds and one year old should sit in a convertible toddler seat in the back of the car.
- After age four and/or 40 pounds and until age eight, children should sit in a booster seat with a seat belt.
- If you have a passenger air bag, don't put your child in the front seat.

CAR PROBLEMS

Report any of the following problems to your mechanic as soon as possible.
- Abnormal readings from gauges
- Brake noise
- Brake-pedal softness or hardness
- Clutch chatter or slipping
- Dashboard warning lights
- Deterioration in ride and handling
- Engine roughness and loss of power
- Exhaust-system roar

- Hard starting
- No horn
- Steering-wheel pull
- Strange engine noise
- Unusual odor
- Vibration
- Windshield wiper streaking

DRIVING WITH A TRAILER

- Take time to practice before driving on main roads.
- Never let anyone ride in or on the trailer.
- Before you leave on a trip, check restrictions on bridges and tunnels.

General Handling

- Use the driving gear that the manufacturer recommends for towing.
- Don't drive fast. Trailer sway is more likely to occur as speed increases.
- Avoid sudden stops and starts. They can cause skidding, sliding or jackknifing.
- Avoid sudden steering actions that might create sway or undue side force on the trailer.
- Slow down when traveling over bumpy roads, railroad crossings and ditches.
- Make wider turns at curves and corners. Because your trailer's wheels are closer to the inside of a turn than the wheels of your tow vehicle, they are more likely to hit or ride up over curbs.
- When a big truck passes from either direction, you may get swaying. That's because of air pressure changes and wind butting.

  Here's what you have to do:

  1. Release the accelerator pedal to slow down.

  2. Keep a firm grip on the steering wheel.

Braking

- Allow considerably more distance for stopping than you would in a car.
- If you have an electric trailer brake controller and excessive sway occurs, activate the trailer brake controller by hand.
- Don't try to control trailer sway by applying the tow vehicle brakes. That will generally make the sway worse.
- Always anticipate the need to slow down. To reduce speed, shift to a lower gear and press the brakes lightly.

Acceleration and Passing

- When passing a slower vehicle or changing lanes, signal well in advance.

Make sure you allow extra distance to clear the vehicle before you pull back into the lane.

- Pass on level terrain with plenty of clearance. Don't pass on steep upgrades or downgrades.
- If necessary, downshift for improved acceleration or to maintain speed.
- When passing on narrow roads, be careful not to go onto a soft shoulder. This could cause your trailer to jackknife or go out of control.

Downgrades and Upgrades

Try not to park on grades.

- Downshift to assist with braking on downgrades and to add power for climbing hills.
- On long downgrades, apply brakes at intervals to keep speed in check. Never leave brakes on for extended periods of time or they may overheat.
- Be sure to use the tow-mode recommended by the manufacturer.

Backing Up

- Put your hand at the bottom of the steering wheel. To turn left, move your hand left. To turn right, move your hand right. Back up slowly.
- Mirrors can't give you all of the visibility you may need when backing up. Have someone outside at the rear of the trailer to guide you, whenever possible.
- Use slight movements of the steering wheel to adjust direction. Exaggerated movements will cause greater movement of the trailer. If you have difficulty, pull forward and realign the tow vehicle and trailer and start again.

Parking

- Try not to park on grades.
- Have someone outside to guide you as you park.
- Once stopped, but before shifting into Park, have someone place blocks on the downhill side of the trailer wheels.
- Apply the parking brake, shift into Park, and then remove your foot from the brake pedal. This parking sequence makes sure your vehicle does not become locked in Park because of an extra load on the transmission. For manual transmissions, first apply the parking brake and then turn the vehicle off in either first or reverse gear.
- When uncoupling a trailer, place blocks at the front and rear of the trailer tires. That's to make sure that the trailer does not roll away when the coupling is released. Before uncoupling, place jack stands under the rear of the trailer to prevent injury. An unbalanced load may cause the tongue to suddenly rotate upward.

114

6 SPORTS INJURIES

When not serious, many sports injuries, including simple sprains and strains, can be treated with "RICE."

RICE stands for —

- Rest the injured area. Do this right away, and keep doing it for 24 to 48 hours. Give the injured part plenty of time to heal before returning to the sports activity.
- Ice the injury. Put a cold compress or an icepack on it for about 15 minutes every hour for the first two or three days, or until the injury no longer feels hot or warm to the touch. After the first 48 hours use a warm compress for 20 minutes three times a day.
- Compress the injury. Wrap it with an elastic bandage for a half hour. Then unwrap it for 15 minutes. People with peripheral vascular disease or diabetes should see a doctor before using an elastic bandage.
- Elevate the injury. Prop it up so it's raised.

To rest the injured part until it gets better, you might want to try a different sport that doesn't put any strain or pressure on the spot. Also ask a trainer about special warm-ups, exercises and stretches.

Be careful. If you are not sure how serious the injury is, treat it as a broken bone. (See page 49.) And, no matter how minor the injury, if pain and discomfort don't go away, or if the area becomes discolored, see a doctor. Don't play through the pain. Don't return to the sport until you've rested and healed.

HEEL SPUR

Also called "plantar fasciitis," this can happen over time to a runner.

WHAT TO LOOK FOR

- Bruising
- Pain in the heel when waking up
- Swelling

WHAT YOU SHOULD DO

1. Stop running, or other sports activity, for the time being.

2. Put a cold compress or ice pack on the heel intermittently for 15 minutes or so. Do this for two days.

3. Elevate foot above level of the heart.

4. After the first 48 hours use a warm compress for 20 minutes three times a day.

5. See a doctor if pain continues or if walking or climbing stairs makes it worse

6. Do not run until you've rested and healed.

IN THE LONG RUN:
- Warm up by doing exercises that stretch calf muscles.
- Avoid running or playing on concrete or other hard terrain.
- Wear the right shoes (no stiff heel).

STRESS FRACTURE (MARCH FRACTURE)

This can happen in the foot when all the weight of the body is suddenly put on the foot bones.

WHAT TO LOOK FOR
- Sharp pain in foot or lower leg   *Always warm up first.*
- Pain when walking

WHAT YOU SHOULD DO
1. Stop the sports activity.

2. Put a cold compress or ice pack on the foot or lower leg intermittently for 15 minutes or so. Do this for two days.

3. Elevate foot above level of the heart.

4. After the first 48 hours, use a warm compress for 20 minutes three times a day.

5. See a doctor.

IN THE LONG RUN:
- Always warm up first.
- Stay away from hard tracks.

SPRAINED ANKLE

This can happen when stepping down hard on the outside of the foot.

WHAT TO LOOK FOR
- Pain
- Popping Sound
- Swelling
- Tearing at side of ankle
- Warm or hot feeling at ankle

WHAT YOU SHOULD DO
1. Stop the sports activity.

2. Put a cold compress or ice pack on the ankle intermittently for 15 minutes or so. Do this for two days.

3. Elevate the foot above the level of the heart.

4. After the first 48 hours, use a warm compress for 20 minutes three times a day.

5. See a doctor if pain continues or gets worse, or if injury comes back, and to make sure a bone hasn't been broken.

IN THE LONG RUN:
- Always warm up first.
- Wear the right shoes for the sport.
- Ask a trainer about taping your ankle to make it more stable.

Don't play through the pain.

RUNNER'S KNEE (PATELLOFEMORAL JOINT PAIN)

This can happen to a runner over time or through a change in running routine.

WHAT TO LOOK FOR
- Pain on or behind kneecap
- Pain while bending knees or squatting
- Pain climbing stairs
- Swelling of the knee
- Popping of the knee

WHAT YOU SHOULD DO
1. Stop the sports activity.

2. Put a cold compress or ice pack on the knee intermittently for 15 minutes or so. Do this for two days.

3. Elevate leg above level of the heart.

4. After the first 48 hours, use a warm compress for 20 minutes three times a day.

5. See a doctor if pain continues or if knee swells up.

IN THE LONG RUN:
- Always warm up first.
- Exercise the quadriceps muscles.
- When biking, try not to use the high gears.

TORN CARTILAGE IN KNEE

A serious twist to the knee when the leg is straightened can cause cartilage in the knee to tear.

WHAT TO LOOK FOR
- Locked or buckling knee
- Pain around knee
- Popping knee
- Swollen knee

WHAT YOU SHOULD DO

1. Stop running.

2. Put a cold compress or ice pack on the knee intermittently for 15 minutes or so. Do this for two days.

3. Keep leg raised.

4. After the first 48 hours, use a warm compress for 20 minutes three times a day.

5. See a doctor if pain continues or if the knee locks or buckles.

IN THE LONG RUN:
- Always warm up first.
- Do exercises to strengthen hamstring and quadriceps muscles.

TORN KNEE LIGAMENT

This can happen in just about any sport.

WHAT TO LOOK FOR
- Pain
- Popping sound
- Stiffness
- Swelling

WHAT YOU SHOULD DO

1. Stop the sports activity.

2. Put a cold compress or ice pack on the knee intermittently for 15 minutes or so.
   a. Do this for two days.

3. Keep leg slightly raised.

4. After the first 48 hours use a warm compress for 20 minutes three times a day.

5. See a doctor if pain continues or if knee swells up.

IN THE LONG RUN:
- Always warm up first.
- Do exercises to strengthen hamstring muscles.

ACHILLES TENDINITIS

Runners can get this tear in the tissue that attaches the calf muscles to the heel bone.

WHAT TO LOOK FOR
- A shooting pain behind the leg just above the ankle
- Swelling

• Tendon may "pop"

WHAT YOU SHOULD DO

1. Stop running.

2. Put a cold compress or ice pack on the painful spot intermittently for 15 minutes or so. Do this for two days.

3. Keep leg slightly raised.

4. After the first 48 hours, use a warm compress for 20 minutes three times a day.

5. See a doctor if pain continues.

IN THE LONG RUN:
• Always warm up first.
• Ask a medical professional about wearing orthotics (shoe inserts).
• Stretch calf muscles and the Achilles tendon with proper exercises.
• Avoid running on hard tracks like concrete.

MUSCLE CRAMPS

This happens when muscles suddenly contract.

WHAT TO LOOK FOR
• Severe pain in muscles

WHAT YOU SHOULD DO

1. Stop the activity.

2. Stretch and squeeze the muscle.

3. Knead, massage or work thumbs into muscle.

4. Place a heating pad or hot water bottle wrapped in a towel on the hurting muscle.

5. Don't resume sport until cramp eases up.

6. See doctor if pain continues.

IN THE LONG RUN:
• Always warm up first.
• Drink plenty of liquids.
• Take it easy in hot weather.
• Add a potassium-rich food like bananas to your diet.

Muscle cramp

HAMSTRING INJURY

This is a tear in the muscles in the back of the thigh that stretch from back of the buttocks to the knee. Basketball players are prone to this injury.

WHAT TO LOOK FOR
- Muscle suddenly tightens up
- Sharp pain in the back of the thigh

WHAT YOU SHOULD DO
1. Stop the sports activity.

2. Put a cold compress or ice pack on the back of the leg intermittently for 15 minutes or so. Do this for two days.

3. Keep leg slightly raised.

4. After the first 48 hours, use a warm compress for 20 minutes three times a day.

5. See a doctor if pain continues or if leg cannot be straightened.

IN THE LONG RUN:
- Always warm up first.
- Strengthen the hamstring and quadriceps muscles with proper exercises.

SHIN SPLINT

This sudden pain in the front of the lower leg often happens to basketball players and can be triggered by running on toes.

WHAT TO LOOK FOR
- Pain in the shin, front and back part of the leg

WHAT YOU SHOULD DO
1. Stop the sports activity.

2. Put a cold compress or ice pack on the front of the lower leg intermittently for 15 minutes or so. Do this for two days.

3. After the first 48 hours, use a warm compress for 20 minutes three times a day.

4. See a doctor if pain continues or if walking becomes difficult.

5. Don't return to running until you've rested and healed.

IN THE LONG RUN:
- Always warm up first.
- Ask a trainer or medical professional about orthotics (shoe inserts).

HIP POINTER

This bruising or muscle tear can happen to athletes when they're hit on or fall on the hip.

WHAT TO LOOK FOR
- Pain in the hip
- Bruising

WHAT YOU SHOULD DO
1. Stop the sports activity.
2. Put a cold compress or ice pack on the hip intermittently for 15 minutes or so. Do this for two days.
3. After the first 48 hours, use a warm compress for 20 minutes three times a day.
4. See a doctor if pain continues or if injury returns.

IN THE LONG RUN:
- Always warm up first.
- Wear hip padding.

LOWER BACK PAIN

This can happen when a muscle is strained or torn, or a disc or vertebra is injured. For instance, a poor golf swing can put heavy pressure on the spine and muscles. This also can bother rowers.

IMPORTANT: *This may be a serious injury and it should be looked at immediately by a medical professional.*

WHAT TO LOOK FOR
- Sharp pain in the lower back and down the backs of the legs
- Slight pull
- Stiffness

WHAT YOU SHOULD DO
1. Stop the sports activity.
2. See a doctor as soon as possible:

    a. If the pain was caused by a blow to the back

    b. If the lower back or legs get numb or begin to tingle

    c. If coughing or sneezing makes the pain worse

3. Go to a hospital ER at once:

    a. If there are problems in urinating or bowel movement

    b. If legs suddenly develop weakness

4. Put an ice compress or pack on the painful spot intermittently for 20 minutes for at least two days.
5. After the first 48 hours use a warm compress for 20 minutes three times a day.

IN THE LONG RUN:
- Always warm up first.
- Do proper stretching exercises before you engage in any sport.

GOLFER'S OR TENNIS ELBOW
- Golfers can get this from a poor downward swing.
- Tennis players can get this from an incorrect backhand stroke or a constant motion of the forearm. Archers and badminton players are also prone to this injury.

WHAT TO LOOK FOR
- Pain on inner side of elbow (golfer's elbow)
- Pain on outer side of elbow (tennis elbow)

WHAT YOU SHOULD DO
1. Stop the sports activity.

2. Put a cold compress or ice pack on the elbow intermittently for 15 minutes or so. Do this for two days.

3. Elevate the elbow above the level of the heart.

4. After the first 48 hours, use a warm, moist compress for 20 minutes three times a day.

5. See a doctor if pain continues or gets worse, or if injury comes back.

IN THE LONG RUN:
- Always warm up first.
- Wear elbow pads when playing.

JAMMED FINGER
This can happen to a baseball player making a bad catch.

WHAT TO LOOK FOR
- Bruising
- Pain
- Swelling

WHAT YOU SHOULD DO
1. Stop playing ball.

2. Put a cold compress or ice pack on the finger intermittently for 15 minutes or so. Do this for two days.

3. Elevate hand above level of the heart.

4. After the first 48 hours, use a warm, moist compress for 20 minutes three times a day.

5. See a doctor if pain continues, if injury comes back, or if you can't straighten your finger.

IN THE LONG RUN:
- Always warm up first.
- Exercise your fingers to strengthen the tendons.

SKIER'S THUMB
A falling skier can sprain a thumb when the strap of the ski pole pulls the thumb away from the fingers.

WHAT TO LOOK FOR
- Pain
- Swelling (puffiness) at base of thumb
- Difficult to pinch or touch pinky with thumb

WHAT YOU SHOULD DO
1. Stop skiing.
2. Put a cold compress or ice pack on the thumb intermittently for 15 minutes or so. Do this for two days.
3. Elevate hand above level of the heart
4. After the first 48 hours, use a warm, moist compress for 20 minutes three times a day.
5. See a doctor if pain continues or if it comes back.

IN THE LONG RUN:
- Always warm up first.
- Exercise your hand to strengthen it.

SWIMMER'S SHOULDER
(PAINFUL ARC, SUBACROMIAL BURSA)
Competitive swimmers are prone to this injury where a shoulder muscle is strained or torn.

WHAT TO LOOK FOR
- Pain in top part of shoulder
- Limited shoulder movement

WHAT YOU SHOULD DO
1. Stop swimming.
2. Put a cold compress or ice pack on the shoulder intermittently for 15 minutes or so. Do this for two days.
3. After the first 48 hours, use a warm, moist compress for 20 minutes three times a day.

4. See a doctor if pain continues or if you can't raise your arm above your head.

IN THE LONG RUN:
- Always warm up first.
- Strengthen shoulder with proper exercises.

SHOULDER SEPARATION OR DISLOCATION
This can be caused by a fall or direct blow to the shoulder.

WHAT TO LOOK FOR
- Bruising
- Bump on shoulder
- Pain in shoulder
- Swelling

Teach kids how to use equipment.

WHAT YOU SHOULD DO
1. Put a sling on the arm.

2. Go to hospital ER immediately.

IN THE LONG RUN:
- The player should wear padding.
- Strengthen shoulder muscles through proper exercises.

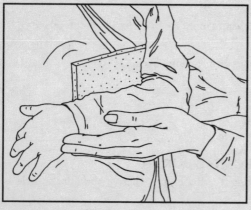

Dislocated Shoulder

SAFETY GUIDE FOR YOUNG ATHLETES
- Make sure they're supervised by adults at all times.
- Give them the right gear in the right size.
- Teach kids how to use equipment.
- Keep the game low key and stress-free to avoid accidents. It's only a game.
- Don't let them play when tired or hurting.
- Always have them warm up before playing.

INDEX

NOTES